PAM GEMS

Amongst many other plays, Pam Gems is the author of *Dusa, Fish, Stas and Vi* (Hampstead and West End), *Queen Christina* (RSC), *Piaf* (RSC, West End and Broadway), *Camille* (RSC and West End), *The Blue Angel* (RSC) and *Deborah's Daughter* (Library Theatre, Manchester). She has produced versions of Chekhov's *Uncle Vanya* and *The Cherry Orchard*, as well as *The Seagull*, and of Ibsen's *A Doll's House* and *Ghosts*. She has also written two novels, *Mrs Frampton* and *Bon Voyage, Mrs Frampton*.

PAM GEMS

DEBORAH'S DAUGHTER

NICK HERN BOOKS
London

A **Nick Hern Book**

Deborah's Daughter first published in 1995
by Nick Hern Books, 14 Larden Road, London W3 7ST

Front cover picture: *Pallas*, pen and ink drawing by Botticelli,
Ashmolean Museum, Oxford

Typeset by Country Setting, Woodchurch, Kent TN26 3TB
Printed by Cox and Wyman, Reading, Berks

A CIP catalogue record for this book is available from
the British Library

ISBN 1 85459 247 5

The god Pluto, who ruled the underworld, stole Persephone, daughter of Demeter, wife of Zeus and goddess of fertility. Demeter, in grief and dispossession, threatened to make the world barren. A compromise was effected.

The Germination of 'Deborah's Daughter'

Of the many poems we studied at grammar school one in parti-
cular, about the myth of Demeter and Persephone, stayed with
me. The story of Pluto, god of the Underworld, who stole
Persephone, daughter of Demeter, the goddess of fertility, and
who agreed to allow her back for part of the year, thus creating
the seasons, lodged in the mind. The form of the poem was regu-
lar and repetitive . . . each stanza ending with 'Persephone . . .
Persephone'. The only other lines I remember are 'A child of
light, a radiant lass, And gamesome as the morning air.' Was it
Browning . . . Tennyson? For some reason, despite meaning to,
I've never sought the source.* Some fragments embed, become
part of you and are yours.

Not that I remember youth as being particularly gamesome.
Growing up between the wars was, for most of us, to live with
exigency. Men stood on street corners, their lovingly ironed
clean collars the humiliating badge of unemployment. There
was little detritus to live on before the full flood of mass
production. Words like 'scrape', 'mend' and 'make do'
encompassed lives. And we were often hungry. Not having
enough to eat can dominate your day.

Many years later, in the sixties, my husband and I managed a
cheap cruise in the Mediterranean on a Greek ship. The cost
was low for a trip all the way to the Lebanon. There was to be
a visit to Jerusalem, for the Holy Sites, and we were to put in
to Egypt – North Africa, where my husband had been for five
years during the war. We had a handsome, moody, Arab
captain, who never smiled. This, said Keith, who had served on
ships, was because our cruise ship was barely seaworthy. At all
events, we never made the Lebanon. Instead, we were holed up
in Alexandria by a vicious Mediterranean storm, where the
food, even in Shepheard's Hotel, tasted of ordure. A trip was
arranged to Cairo where, held up in traffic, I saw a young lad
in a ragged djellabah dodge into the gutter under our wheels to

pick a dying lettuce leaf out of horse manure. And eat it. As we left Cairo, on our right were houses, streets and gardens. On our left, desert. As far as the eye could see. All the way to the Atlantic.

It is out of fragments of experience that work is born. The idea of being a tourist can certainly be dented by the sight of a child so hungry that he will eat a dying, filthy leaf. It is said that tourism has global benefit, that it brings wealth to the Third World, as does western style business. Together with disadvantages. That may well be true. What we do know is that the world now has the technology to solve our physical problems. We can feed ourselves, all of us, if we want to.

Pam Gems

* I had a cordial letter from Barry Harkison, of Manchester, who solved the mystery of the poem. It is by the Victorian poet Jean Ingelow. He writes: 'What may interest you is that it was written in January 1862 as part of Ingelow's involvement in a largely women's group called The Portfolio Society. The subject the poets gave themselves was Light and Shade and Adelaide Procter also write a poem on the topic (but not about this myth).' This is most interesting as *Deborah's Daughter* was produced as part of the season of drama in Manchester, and as a contribution to The Year of the Family. It was most cordially received except by two London critics who took offence at the love scenes, finding them 'embarrassing'. It's not often you feel sorry for critics. Readers, they haven't lived.

Deborah's Daughter was first performed at the Library
Theatre, Manchester on 3 March 1994 with the following cast:

DEBORAH PEDERSEN	Anna Carteret
RHODA, LADY WIGGINS	Jane Freeman
STEPHANIE PEDERSEN	Mia Fothergill
HASSAN SA'ID IBN SA'ID	Raad Rawi
ERIC BELLAIRS	Peter Yapp
DAVID DELAVIGNE	Philip Darling
ALI MADUR	Nasser Memarzia
SOLDIER / YUSUF	Royce Hounsell

Directed by Sue Dunderdale
Designed by Shimon Castiel
Lighting Designer Jim Simmons

Characters

DEBORAH PEDERSEN, in her forties.

STEPHANIE PEDERSEN, Deborah's daughter, who is just seventeen.

RHODA, Lady Wiggins, Deborah's mother, an old Africa hand.

ERIC BELLAIRS, MI6.

DAVID DELAVIGNE, a young man of stable background.

HASSAN. Sa'id Ibn Sa'id, an army colonel.

ALI MADUR, captain and aide to Hassan.

Act One, Scene One

We are outside the army headquarters of the last sizeable town in the south of a north African country. A podium has been set up. Bright sunlight, and a stiff breeze which blows the scarves and dresses of the women sitting on the row of formal chairs behind the standing microphone. They are STEPHANIE, very young, with shining fair hair, wearing a simple white dress. RHODA, elderly, in sweet-pea colours, with an old safari jacket over and a cloth hat. And, next to a heavily built Arab in army uniform, DEBORAH PEDERSEN. She is a comely woman, with an expressive face. She grimaces a good deal, often in self-deprecation. She sits awkwardly, legs twisted under her chair, her hair in disarray under a deceptively simple hat. Her clothes seem to flow and loop about her, giving her a muddled but attractive appearance. She draws you. You want to rescue her.

Also on the platform is ERIC BELLAIRS, officiating from the British Consulate, a thin, dark man of middle age, and DAVID DELAVIGNE, an attractive and energetic young man in chinos, who is videoing the scene. CAPTAIN ALI MADUR, the colonel's aide, cranes offstage, waves a hand. There is a slight hiatus, and then, very loud on the P/A, the country's national anthem. The COLONEL and the CAPTAIN stand to attention, ERIC BELLAIRS likewise. DEBORAH scoops at her hair. The group makes to sit but the music resurges, catching them out. As it stops RHODA sits firmly.

ALI (*at the microphone, in Arabic*). People, gather . . . Come close . . .

ERIC (*leans over to DEBORAH*). Your turn Mrs. Pedersen.

He helps her up with an encouraging smile.

DEBORAH *rises, ascends the podium.* CAPTAIN MADUR *stands by, with his own hand-held microphone.*

DEBORAH (*in Arabic*). Hail to the great and wise King Jawal bin Jadal. Would that he might be among us. (*In English*.) Ladies and gentlemen, I bring greetings to His Majesty, King Jawal, by whose benevolent permission this ceremony takes place.

ALI *translates into Arabic. Some booing. The* COLONEL *glares.*

I am here on behalf of my husband, Per Pedersen, whose loss has been grievous not only to me but to this country. (*She waits as* ALI *translates.*) In his memory . . . (ALI *translates.*) . . . As a token of the deep attachment between Pedersen Oil and your historic country . . . (ALI *translates.*) . . . And in the sure hope that we may continue to co-operate and prosper together . . . (ALI *translates.*) . . . I offer this gift of fifty million dollars . . . (*Clapping from the platform.* ALI *translates. Loud clapping and cheers and ululation from the audience.*) The money is to be used to make the desert flourish, and I am honoured to be your president in this vital venture. (ALI *makes to translate, but she goes on. He looks at his copy of the speech, baffled.*) My mother . . . (*She turns to* RHODA, *who squints up at her impassively.*) . . . As you all know, my mother, Lady Wiggins, is an old Africa hand and –

RHODA (*growls*). Not that old –

DEBORAH. I myself was attached to your Royal Institute as a consulting agricultural biologist, before my marriage. In those days we had such hopes, with new varieties suited to . . . And now . . . With the drought . . . Ohh . . .

ERIC, *worried, rises.*

I've . . . I have been so very deeply concerned – but, believe me, there is nothing – nothing we cannot achieve – if we can just get the water in, the desert will flourish – (ERIC *looks perturbed.*) . . . It *can* . . . It *must* – I'm sorry . . . (*She sways slightly. It seems as though she may collapse but the* COLONEL'*s arms are immediately and strongly about her.*) Thank you . . . Thank you I'm . . . (*She pulls away from him sharply and he lets her go at once.*) Thank you.

DAVID (*hisses*). Mrs. Pedersen . . . The cheque . . .

She turns to ERIC *who gives her the cheque. She waves it uncertainly towards the* COLONEL *who clicks a finger for a* CAPTAIN *bearing a silver salver who steps forward and comes to attention.* DEBORAH *places the cheque on the salver. It immediately blows away. The* CAPTAIN *bends, retrieves the cheque, wipes it on his ass delicately to remove the sand and anchors it to the salver with his thumb. Then turns, and bears away the cheque with proud formality, changing step twice to be in time with the band which has now resurged. The* COLONEL *turns, bows deeply to* DEBORAH *to applause, and kisses her hand. She retrieves her hand with difficulty. Over the appallingly played Souza march* RHODA *cups her hands and bawls at the* COLONEL.

RHODA. Hassan! Get them to shut up! (*The* COLONEL *comes to her side and bends to listen. She bawls again.*) Tell them to pack it in, will you?

The COLONEL *nods. He waves a slack hand and the band stops in mid-note. He steps forward, nods briefly. The sound of military commands, a drum roll, the sound of men coming very raggedly to attention. Silence. The* COLONEL *turns to* DEBORAH *who backs away circumspectly.*

RHODA. Thank God for that.

HASSAN (*smiles, looking even more a brigand*). For you, beloved Umm, as brief as possible. (*Kisses* RHODA's *hand.*)

DEBORAH (*apart, to* STEPHANIE). I do wish he wouldn't do that.

STEPHANIE. Mummy, it's probably the custom, he doesn't mean anything.

DEBORAH. Oh I think he does.

ERIC. Went very well, Colonel. (*Seeing* HASSAN *loom towards* DEBORAH *he draws him away, shaking his hand firmly.*)

DAVID (*to* STEPHANIE). Is your mother OK?

STEPHANIE. It's just the heat. It makes her dizzy.

DAVID. She's looking great.

STEPHANIE (*as he takes still shots*). Oh dear, do you think
    so? (*She regards her mother doubtfully.*) When my father
    was alive she always looked splendid . . . Now, I don' t
    know

DAVID (*packing his gear*). Don't worry, it'll all be edited.

ERIC. We'd better go in – (DAVID *and* STEPHANIE *look up
    in enquiry.*) – there's a small reception.

RHODA. Not another, Eric!

ERIC. This one's our show . . . I've kept it very brief.

RHODA. Good!

ERIC. Rather an elaborate do tonight, I'm afraid . . . The local
    heat were insistent. Ah – (*Again he forestalls the
    COLONEL, who makes to escort DEBORAH. She backs
    away with a nervous smile.*) Colonel Sa'id – I hear there's a
    Mozart trio tonight!

STEPHANIE. Mozart? In the desert? (*She is enchanted by the
    idea.*)

RHODA. Very recherché, Hassan. Direct from Old Vienna?

HASSAN (*with a morose scowl*). From Libya.

RHODA. Hah! (*She cackles with laughter. He shakes his head
    at her, a warning.*)

HASSAN. Goodwill tour. (*This makes RHODA laugh
    genuinely. He turns on DEBORAH suddenly, making her
    jump.*) And for this lady . . . one thousand roses!

DEBORAH. I'm sorry, were you talking to me?

HASSAN. White roses! grown in the cool hills, in secret
    groves, for the honour of our beloved benefactor. Tell me,
    is this, in the female, benefactress? I would wish, most
    sincerely, not to give offence by desexing your good self.

(*He laughs loudly and grasps her by the elbow.*) My English is affluent, is it not?

DEBORAH. On the contrary, I should say it was wilfully rotten. Are you coming in? (To STEPHANIE.)

She goes inside, to the reception, with STEPHANIE *and* DAVID.

RHODA (*mutters*). Hassan, that's enough.

HASSAN. Mere social intercourse.

RHODA. You won't get much intercourse there.

ERIC. Colonel, I have to confess . . . Talking of . . . ah –

HASSAN (*genial*). Mister Bellairs?

ERIC. Nothing. Just wondering about – the need for all this. Surely everything could have been arranged in London. If you remember, we suggested informal talks in the country at Mrs. Pedersen's home. She would have been so much more comfortable –

HASSAN. Nah, nah, nah . . . different world. Important she is here.

ERIC. Why? There's nothing that couldn't –

HASSAN. I have watched this lady. In London she is not happy. She shudders at her responsibility. She wishes to be the child, to be obedient.

ERIC. In London she has the direct advice and support of her consortium. We could have managed the business simply, without delay. Our joint interests could –

HASSAN. Nah, nah, nah, nah, nah. The Pedersen consortium . . . you know its structure . . . Many associates . . . Japan . . . America . . .

ERIC. We've been given assurances –

HASSAN. Assurances for you. Not for us.

ERIC. Nonetheless, to bring the widow here – I still fail to –

RHODA. It was my suggestion! (*Pulls a face at* ERIC.)

HASSAN. Lady Wiggins wishes for her daughter a more direct connection with this country of her financial concern.

RHODA. And don't forget I wangled it, Hassan. I shall expect a quid pro quo. (*He looks at her gloomily.*)

HASSAN. If Mrs. Pedersen can witness for herself the lives of those she –

ERIC. Ye-es. Perhaps. Though I still can't quite . . . however, here we are. No doubt our mutual interests can continue to be successfully served.

RHODA. Split infinitive, Eric.

ERIC. Thank you, Rhoda. (*He takes* HASSAN *aside.*) Any minute now the Foreign Office are going to get shirty, I've no official authority for any of this. As you know. How long is this thing going to take?

HASSAN. Immediate. I guarantee. (ERIC *makes to speak.*) I am suggesting a visit. To the south.

ERIC. Is that necessary? Advisable? (HASSAN *gives him a stone-faced look.*) She's already – the grain donation was at her insistence and I believe the consortium has approved further funding for lorries and medical supplies. She's very fragile. You might be wise not to push your –

HASSAN. One visit then, to the excavation – for morale.

RHODA. Just the thing, she needs a jolly good –

ERIC (*sweetly*). Shut up,

RHODA (*to* HASSAN). Is it safe?

HASSAN (*shrugs*). Probably.

RHODA. Safer than anywhere else in –

ERIC. Sorry, can't take the risk. If this thing comes to the boil I need your assurance, immediate escort out of here, in fact I'm not sure it wouldn't be wisest to cut events short after tonight, continue at arms length.

RHODA. Nonsense, you love to live dangerously. Come on, whisky and soda.

HASSAN. No risk, I assure you.

ERIC. I have your word?

HASSAN. Of course, of course, of course.

RHODA. Go on, show her the irrigation, Hassan. Do her the world of good. (*She hands* ERIC *her old music case, they stroll off together*). Well, Eric, and how's life these days? Still dabbling?

ERIC. Alas, all too rarely. One lives in hopes.

RHODA. Saw Mustapha last week.

ERIC (*pleased*). Oh? Did you? How is he?

RHODA. Very well. Sends his love.

> *They exit.* HASSAN, *alone, gazes out at the desert. A dog barks.* STEPHANIE *enters quietly, making him jump.*

HASSAN (*abrupt*). What? I'm sorry, I didn't see you.

STEPHANIE. They're waiting . (*He shrugs, indifferent. She approaches and joins him. They look out at the desert.*)

STEPHANIE (*softly*). I've never seen anything like it.

HASSAN (*looks at her briefly*). The desert?

STEPHANIE. So many colours! I thought it would be like . . . Bournemouth beach. Grey . . . Orange . . . Pink . . .

HASSAN. The hills are full of copper . . . Aluminium. It ruins reception, when you want a weather report. (*He gazes out at the desert, abstracted.*)

STEPHANIE. No green, of course. (*He doesn't reply.*) At home everything's green – green fields, green trees . . . green cows . . .

> *This does get his attention. He turns, frowning.*
> STEPHANIE *points.*

Look – over there – that peak. Violet.

HASSAN (*softly*). 'The violets in the mountain have split the rock.'

STEPHANIE. That's Tennessee Williams! How surprising. I mean, for a soldier. To read poetry.

HASSAN. It is not unknown.

STEPHANIE. Do you carry a slim volume in your knapsack?

HASSAN. Of course. Under the hand grenades.

STEPHANIE. You know, you're going to have to do something about that.

HASSAN. About what?

STEPHANIE. The sneer. (*He looks at her neutrally.*) Every time you say something to us. I mean, I do understand, but we're not -- speaking for myself, I didn't ask to be born Stephanie Pedersen, only daughter of a . . . what-do-you-call – it – a tycoon. It can interfere with your freedom, believe me.

HASSAN. I am sure.

STEPHANIE. We're not drones, you know! Mummy and I work very hard on the farm. We're very efficient, my mother has a trained mind and we're totally organic.

HASSAN (*laughs*). Yes, I can see that.

STEPHANIE. Honestly, you really are the most terrible flirt, Hassan. I don't mind for myself, but it puts the wind up Mummy no end.

HASSAN. She is not organic?

STEPHANIE. Stop it. She's splendid. We use no chemicals, no phosphates, no artificial nitrogen on the land, and no machinery. Heavy machinery destroys soil structure.

HASSAN. No machinery? No oil, no petrol? (*She shakes her head, laughing.*) And your name is Pedersen?

STEPHANIE. I know! Bizarre, isn't it? Don't tell the share holders. You could farm like this here, it's much cheaper and just as efficient – we do just as well as conventional farmers – well, no-one's thriving at the moment, it's a bad time. We're lucky, we have the flowers.

HASSAN, *who has been looking at her, enjoying her youth and beauty without listening, frowns.*

HASSAN. Flowers?

STEPHANIE. You should see them! . . . Acres and acres and acres . Mummy's a famous breeder.

HASSAN. Of flowers?

STEPHANIE. Bulbs mainly. We export all over the world. She's famous for it.

HASSAN *looks out over the desert.*

HASSAN. You grow flowers.

Slight pause.

STEPHANIE. Yes, I suppose that does sound frivolous here.

He looks at her gloomily.

England's so different! In Hereford everything's wet . . . moist – things grow all the time! Everything's fertile.

She looks at him. He stares at the desert.

STEPHANIE. Just the same, you do have things that we don't.

HASSAN. We have nothing.

STEPHANIE. You have this. All this . . . beauty. (*Slight pause.*) I'm sorry. We've been reading about the drought in the south. We saw the pictures. My mother is very distressed.

HASSAN. Our gratitude knows no depths. We are moved by her intervention.

STEPHANIE. You're doing it again! (*Slight pause.*) What will happen to the money? I mean if –

HASSAN. We shall divert the river, as agreed.

STEPHANIE. You'll go ahead with it – afterwards? (*He looks round carefully.*) No-one can hear us. (*Slight pause. She looks round.*) What are all the soldiers waiting for?

HASSAN *follows her glance, looks round idly.*

HASSAN. For me to dismiss them.

STEPHANIE. Shouldn't you do so?

HASSAN (*absently, enjoying her company*). Oh, I don't know. (*She laughs.*) What?

STEPHANIE. You can be lovely sometimes. I must go. Mummy's not well. (*She dances off backwards, calls as she disappears.*) Claustrophobial . . .

HASSAN. Here? In the desert? (*He watches her go, then shouts, in Arabic.*) Remove this rabble of untrained petty delinquents and breakers of their mother's hearts.

Shrieked commands in Arabic. The sound of men coming raggedly to attention. Another shriek, the men fall out and run off across the asphalt. ALI enters, salutes. He and HASSAN walk apart, in close discussion. They look serious. ALI listens as HASSAN gives him instructions. HASSAN leaves. ALI makes to leave separately, pauses as DEBORAH, in seeming agitation, hurries on.

DEBORAH. Stephanie – Stephanie, are you there?

ALI. Madame?

DEBORAH (*nervous*). What?

ALI. May I help you?

DEBORAH. No. Yes, I'm looking for my daughter.

ALI. Please, allow me – (*He tries to usher her off.*)

DEBORAH. No, I –

STEPHANIE (*off*). Mother?

DEBORAH. Stephanie? Where is she, what have you – (*She sees STEPHANIE.*) – oh there you are! I was looking for you, I didn't know where you were!

She rushes off, sending ALI reeling. Alone, he talks urgently in Arabic into a mobile telephone.

Act One, Scene Two

A terrace at one of the ruler's palatial winter residences. Low seating, in the Moorish style, lavishly appointed. Low, decorated tables, and softly lit lamps. In the background, the sound of the Mozart trio.

DAVID *enters in a dinner jacket. He looks round for* STEPHANIE, *goes off to find her, hands in pockets, whistling to himself cheerfully.*

A slight pause. STEPHANIE *enters in a diaphanous green and cream gauze dress, girdled with narrow gold. She looks like a young nymph. Thinking herself alone she turns, swaying, to the music. She dances for a few moments, then goes off towards the sound of the music.*

HASSAN, *resplendent in Arab robes, emerges from the shadows.* ALI *enters and they walk apart, talking urgently in Arabic.* HASSAN *breaks away, angry at* ALI'*s news.*

HASSAN (*in Arabic*). Not one guarantee of support?

ALI. On attend, mon Colonel. They will wait.

> ERIC, *in evening clothes, enters, and catches* HASSAN'*s grimace of fury. He looks from one to the other.*

ERIC (*politely*). Any news?

ALI (*bows respectfully*). Mr. Bellairs.

> ERIC *looks from one to the other. They stare at him sombrely.*

ERIC. I see. No further support. Are you saying nothing, not even from your own – ?

ALI. No sir. Our brothers in the north prefer to wait on events.

HASSAN (*savagely*). They will wait.

> *A pause.*

ERIC. So it's off? (*Silence.*) You can't mean that you – ?

HASSAN. We move anyway.

Silence. ERIC *shakes his head vigorously.*

ERIC. Try the Russians. Why not? they're flogging everything to anyone! (*The Arabs look at him sternly.*)

ALI. For dollars, Mr. Bellairs. For dollars. (*Softly.*) We have no dollars.

HASSAN (*turns, he has decided*). We move.

ERIC (*prompt*). In that case I need a safe conduct out of here tonight.

HASSAN. Why? Everything is under control –

The music stops. Clapping.

ERIC (*raising his voice*). Not if you jump the gun it isn't – (*Lowers his voice as the clapping stops.*) Now listen, I insist –

ALI. Les femmes –

ERIC. Qui? Oh.

ALI *indicates off as* RHODA *enters quickly.*

RHODA. There you are, Hassan. (*Low.*) Any news? Damn. (*As* DEBORAH *enters behind her.*)

DEBORAH. Mother, you're wrong . . . it was Teignmouth, I knew I was right! (*Her voice falters as* STEPHANIE, *coming towards her, sees* HASSAN *and crosses to him.*) I remember it most distinctly . . . (*Her voice trails off, then she recovers her attention.*) We were standing at the water's edge, and the church clock struck five and I looked up and suddenly everything – sea, sand, sky . . . everything dissolved into this golden opalescence. I thought it was my condition, I was carrying Stephanie at the time.

ERIC. Oh, Teignmouth can be like that in the late afternoon. Turner painted what he saw.

HASSAN *and* STEPHANIE *stroll off.* DEBORAH *is agitated.*

DEBORAH (*calls*). Stephanie – !

RHODA. Let her go.

DEBORAH. Oh!

RHODA. You never said you knew Devon, Eric.

ERIC. Yes I did. I told you everyone talked of a Lady Wiggins –

RHODA. That was me! –

ERIC. . . . a young society woman – when I was a boy –

RHODA. – just after I married Gervase –

ERIC. – known as a great beauty – the Rose of Devonshire

RHODA. Me! before I took to the drink.

DEBORAH (*as they go*). Mother, do be quiet. (*A pause. Piano music, soft, offstage, a Chopin nocturne.* HASSAN *and* STEPHANIE *stroll.*)

HASSAN (*amused*). Beauty . . . a human necessity? Why?

   STEPHANIE *shrugs, uncertain, searches for an answer.*

STEPHANIE. It keeps us going?

HASSAN. And you believe it advisable, to keep going?

STEPHANIE. That rather depends on the alternatives.

HASSAN. What if risk is the only choice?

STEPHANIE. Oh Hassan! I know! And you know what I feel, you know I believe in the things we talked about, the night we talked all night! Just the same . . . Just the same there *are* advantages to gradualism.

HASSAN. Name one.

STEPHANIE. A lower body count?

HASSAN. I am a soldier –

STEPHANIE. So you believe in killing people.

HASSAN. If necessary.

STEPHANIE. In destroying life.

HASSAN. And you are prepared always to submit?

STEPHANIE. In bending to the wind, yes. Not very brave, I admit, but a good wheeze for surviving.

HASSAN. Hah!

STEPHANIE (*picking up on his urgency*). There are other ways!

HASSAN. Such as?

STEPHANIE. Subversion . . . Persuasion . . .

HASSAN. You think people fight for pleasure?

STEPHANIE. Yes! At first, anyway . . . burn it, smash it up – most people lead boring, boring lives! They need . . . well, it's what I've read. People need challenge. They like change. We're programmed for it.

HASSAN. But you prefer the predictable.

STEPHANIE. I like to know where I stand, yes.

HASSAN. Watch me. (*He blows.*) There. What do you see?

STEPHANIE. Nothing.

HASSAN. Yet I have changed the world. (*Offstage, dance music begins softly.*) I blow . . . (*He blows again.*) . . . And air is displaced around the whole world. This must be so. (*Dance music.*)

STEPHANIE (*laughs, blows*). There, I've blown it all back again.

DEBORAH. You seem to be enjoying yourselves. (*Enters with DAVID.*)

DAVID. Steffie, want to dance?

STEPHANIE. Ooh, please! (*To HASSAN.*) Excuse me. (*She runs off.*)

DEBORAH. My daughter seems quite taken with you, Colonel Sa'id.

HASSAN. She is intelligent.

DEBORAH. And very young still. In England girls don't develop quite so early.

HASSAN. She is old enough to make children – please, sit down.

DEBORAH. Ah, no, I . . .

HASSAN. Please. Captain, for the lady if you would – whisky and soda? Gin and it?

He waves DEBORAH to a low cushioned seat where she sits, knees primly together. ALI appears, both men bend solicitously over her.

DEBORAH. Nothing, thank you . (*As ALI continues to loom.*) A glass of Evian. (*ALI looks baffled.*) Fruit juice . . . Anything.

Over her head HASSAN nods meaningfully to ALI.

ALI. Madame. (*He bows and goes. Slight pause.*)

DEBORAH. You must forgive my anxiety, Colonel. My daughter is my only child, and naturally we've had to protect her – there is always the wretched fear of kidnapping.

HASSAN. I am aware.

His voice is soft, compassionate. It makes her look at him directly.

HASSAN. You are her mother. (*He holds her glance.*)

DEBORAH (*slightly out of face*). This is her first time in Africa. Naturally she – her imagination is bound to be stimulated.

HASSAN. And you, Madame?

DEBORAH. I beg your pardon?

HASSAN. May we hope that you, too, perhaps –

DEBORAH. No, no, no. (*Flustered under his intense gaze.*) This isn't my first visit. I worked here before, as a research scientist, before my marriage.

HASSAN. And you are much respected.

DEBORAH. It was a long time ago –

HASSAN. Revered! (*He leans forward, murmurs sensuously.*) I have read your paper on short-stemmed wheat.

DEBORAH (*removing his hand from her knee*). Most of my work was on maize.

HASSAN. I know! Jumping genes! The gene in the maize kernel which leaps, unbidden, from chromosome to chromosome. (*He stands, declares.*) 'Transposable Elements' by Doctor Deborah Wiggins! You see? – I have your book.

DEBORAH. Really? (*For a moment she shines up at him but then pulls a face.*) It's out of date now. I'm just a geneticist. It's all molecular biology these days, ever since Crick and Watson and Kendrew. And Rosy – Rosy Franklin of course. And Linus Pauling in America.

HASSAN. But you don't lose the passion? The desire?

DEBORAH. For science? How could I? For some of us science is poetry.

HASSAN. Then why not return?

DEBORAH. No, no. Much too late.

HASSAN. Why not? Everything is possible.

DEBORAH (*shakes her head*). I'd have to retrain, begin again. (*But she hugs her legs wistfully, like a girl.*) I still miss it, all that wonderful work on moulds, spores and fungi. (*She sighs deeply.*) I gave up when I married.

HASSAN (*barks*). Why?

DEBORAH. Because – it was impossible. My husband's life was extremely demanding. He needed me to . . . I was needed.

HASSAN. For what? To extract from the earth more oil?

DEBORAH. We can hardly do without it, Colonel.

HASSAN *slaps his thigh loudly, shouts with laughter, making her jump.*

HASSAN. But you do . . . you do!

DEBORAH. I'm sorry?

HASSAN. You do, lady! Your daughter tells me that you spurn the use of oil, the source of all your fortune.

DEBORAH. What? Oh, you mean on the farm! Now that is something I *would* like to discuss while we are here. The need to conserve world resources is absolutely vital – don't you agree?

HASSAN. Yes, yes. So we must live modestly as the West tells us, with the loom and the donkey, like Mr. Gandhi. Very picturesque, especially for the tourists. Our people are dying.

DEBORAH. Yes, Colonel, I know! And that is precisely why the diversion of this river is so vital. Top soil, Colonel Sa'id – top soil! the secret of fertility.

HASSAN. From one small river.

DEBORAH. A beginning. You're too pessimistic – have faith!

HASSAN. Easy for you. You are white, you are rich. That which you choose you can have.

DEBORAH. And you can have fruit and vegetables growing in the sand in a year. Believe me. Look at the plans, they're of the utmost simplicity. All of our work is based on the practical.

HASSAN. A simple plan for simple people.

DEBORAH. No human being is simple. (*She turns, catches his gaze, for a moment they are held, then she looks away.*) As for being rich, my daughter and I live very plainly.

HASSAN. You play the shepherdess. Very pretty.

DEBORAH. We choose to conserve.

HASSAN. And you have never considered that in a position of such privilege more may be required of you than to ape poverty? Mrs Pedersen – (*As she tries to interrupt.*) – you occupy position of power.

DEBORAH. Which I have never sought to use.

HASSAN. Why not?

DEBORAH. That was my husband's world.

HASSAN. Your husband is dead. (*Pause. Softly.*) You will
come to the Rift?

DEBORAH. Not this time. Perhaps later

HASSAN. A disappointment. No doubt you have other
diversions.

DEBORAH. I have other calls on my time, yes.

HASSAN. They have dug into the ground for you.

DEBORAH. Really, Colonel, I can hardly believe that my visit
would be anything other than an interruption. I'm unlikely to
contribute by standing over the earth-movers in person –
besides, it's too hot.

HASSAN. My house is built on water. It is a fortress of El
Glaoui. There are pools, and trees, and many beautiful
flowers. Please. This would be for us great pleasure. And
for the children.

DEBORAH. Your family?

HASSAN. The children of the village. I have no family.

DEBORAH (*surprised*). You're not married?

ALI *appears with a large silver tray with drinks. He puts a
tall glass at* DEBORAH'*s elbow and fills it from a silver
pitcher. He serves* HASSAN *with whisky, then presents a
large, apricot-coloured velvet box of sweets, opening it with
reverent ceremony and placing it by* DEBORAH'*s elbow
with a formal bow. He bows again and goes.* DEBORAH
lifts her glass politely to HASSAN.

DEBORAH. Well, ah . . . your health. (*She sips, drinks again.*)
Mmm . . . it's rather pleasant. You were saying you were not
married, Colonel?

HASSAN. My wife is dead. For seven years I have lived alone.

DEBORAH. Seven years? That's a long time. (*She drinks and he refills her glass.*) Believe me, I understand loss. (*He leans forward, offers her the box of sweets. She shakes her head.*) No thank you.

HASSAN. A special gift from His Majesty – apricot and almond.

DEBORAH. Oh – well . . . (*She takes one. He waits expectantly so she tastes it.*) Thank you . . . It's very nice.

HASSAN (*slaps his thigh*). Good – we don't chop off the hand of the chef!

DEBORAH. I don't find that very amusing, Colonel Sa'id.

HASSAN. No doubt you have read of torture in our prisons.

DEBORAH. It's in the world press.

HASSAN. And what do you think? (*But he slaps his thigh again, speaks heartily.*) But now is not the time for political discussion, heh? Social occasion! Time for celebration of your so generous gift. Madame . . . your health. Santé.

They both drink. Slight pause. DEBORAH *puts down her glass.*

DEBORAH. How did you . . . ah . . . come to lose your wife?

HASSAN. Somebody blew her feet off.

DEBORAH. Oh! (*Shocked, she can find nothing to say.*) I'm sorry. (*She picks up her glass, drinks deep.*)

HASSAN. I have known women, of course. But all dark.

He leans forward. DEBORAH *draws back.*

You see, Mrs. Pedersen, I look to the light. (*He moves closer to her.*) Your skin is translucent, do you know that? Like wax, at an altar.

He bends, looks up into her face.

You permit?

He kisses her forearm. She jumps up as if shot.

DEBORAH (*with a little shriek*). Colonel Sa'id!

HASSAN. Please . . .

DEBORAH. That's enough!

STEPHANIE (*off*). Mother, are you all right?

DEBORAH (*calls*). No – yes! (*Hisses to* HASSAN.) I don't
know what you think you're doing –

HASSAN. Please, sit down.

DEBORAH (*sitting heavily*). Certainly not.

HASSAN. Forgive me. You are so beautiful.

DEBORAH (*becoming garrulous with the fruit cup*). Rubbish,
I'm a sick and tiresome woman and you couldn't possibly
find me attractive so if, for whatever motive, you seek to
flirt with me, I can tell you now it'll be woefully disap-
pointing, I've no talent for that sort of thing, none at all.
I suppose you think all European women are the same, free
with their . . . but it's by no means – in my case I must tell
you that . . . (*She refills her glass, drinks, slams down the
glass.*) . . . For God's sake what have they put in this drink,
it's revolting!

HASSAN. Please, sit down. Allow me to – ach!

DEBORAH. Ow! (*As they bump heads.*) I beg your pardon –

HASSAN. I am sorry –

DEBORAH. Not at all, it was my fault. I'm a mass of nerves.

HASSAN. No. No. You are a lily. A slender lily, full of
promise –

DEBORAH. A repository for medication, you mean.

HASSAN. No, no, no. Your body is most sacred.

DEBORAH. My body, Colonel Sa'id, is a founder member of
Depressives Anonymous. Or was. The others have all
topped themselves or been committed but then, what would
you know about that, no doubt you spend your days between
the parade ground and the torture chamber –

HASSAN. Your arms . . . I cannot believe your arms. They gleam like pale wands of peeled willow –

DEBORAH (*frantically trying to divert him as he closes on her*). Willow? . . . Does that grow here, it's a widely diversified species –

HASSAN. You smell of hyacinth. (*Dance music changes to a tango.*)

DEBORAH. Diorissimo . . . it's Diorissimo . . .

HASSAN (*murmurs*). Goddess of light . . .

He kisses her. She starts to struggle but is overwhelmed by the sensation. She drowns. At last he draws back. The music stops.

DEBORAH. Now look what you've done. Oh please . . .

He kisses her again.

What on earth can you want with me?

HASSAN (*murmurs*). What on earth?

He bends and kisses the inside of her forearm.

DEBORAH. No, stop it. (*She walks away from him to a safe distance.*) What is it you want? Don't tell me you'd like to throw me across your saddle and ride off into the desert?

HASSAN. Of course. Please . . .

DEBORAH. No!

HASSAN. Why not?

DEBORAH. I don't have to give you a reason. (*She fishes wildly in her evening bag, trying to find a comb. Finds it and rakes at her hair, looking into the mirror of her powder compact.*) If you want a woman, get a wife – you're allowed four, aren't you? To treat as you please since we're not supposed to have souls in your religion . . . What's the catchphrase? – Islamic heaven, where women are numerous, available and never menstruate? (*She sits on the floor.*) I'm drunk. (*He sits down beside her.*)

HASSAN. You find me ugly?

DEBORAH *scrambles very awkwardly to her feet.*

DEBORAH (*shouting*). Oh! I see! Now he wants reassurance!

HASSAN. Please, don't shout –

DEBORAH. I'm not shouting!

DEBORAH *spins, slightly giddy, and sits apart from HASSAN on the low seat. She speaks with studied dignity.*

DEBORAH. Colonel. I have obviously, and quite unintentionally, given you a completely wrong impression –

HASSAN. Not at all, it is I who must beg your forgiveness. (*He straightens his robes fastidiously.*) I shall resign from the army in the morning.

DEBORAH. Oh don't talk rubbish.

HASSAN. I have dishonoured you. I must be punished for this crime.

DEBORAH. Nonsense, don't be so silly. It was only a . . . an . . . I'm prepared to forget the whole thing.

HASSAN. I have insulted you.

DEBORAH. No I'm not, I'm not insulted, I've just said so, as you see, I'm not even angry. I shall . . . I shall accept it as a compliment and we'll let it go at that.

HASSAN. Good, and you will come to the Rift tomorrow?

DEBORAH. I'm sorry, no.

HASSAN. The men work hard into the night to dig for you. Please, so little to ask from one who has so much.

DEBORAH. I'm sorry, I can't.

HASSAN. Why not?

DEBORAH. For one thing because I feel so ill all the time!

HASSAN. No. You will not be ill. In my house, in my garden, you will be well. Say that you will come. Please . . . I ask from the heart. (*He gazes down at her, close.*) It will be pleasure for you. I, Hassan, promise it.

DEBORAH. Oh, I see – a treat! Thank you so much . . . so grateful! Strutting around knowing we're all looking at him in . . . (*She waves at his robes, stumbles over a stool.*) . . . And this great prick of a house . . . columns . . . court-yards . . . who organised tonight, it wasn't on our schedule –

HASSAN. It was arranged for you, for your pleasure –

DEBORAH. For me? *My* pleasure? (*Laughs wildly.*) Oh, where oh where have I heard *that* before! (*She stumbles against another footstool, boots it across the room.*)

STEPHANIE (*off, calls*). Mummy, are you all right?

DEBORAH (*bawls*). Yes!! (*She lowers her voice.*) I would have you know that I am not some – accessory . . . appendage . . . (*He proffers the box of sweets. She knocks them out of his hands.*) – and I don't eat sweets!

HASSAN *scrabbles for the sweets.*

HASSAN. I ask only small favour . . .

DEBORAH. I am my own man now. I shall do as I please.

HASSAN *rises, puts down the box of sweets.*

HASSAN (*softly*). And as you desire?

DEBORAH *looks at him soberly.*

DEBORAH. At all events, Colonel Sa'id, I don't desire conquest. That's where we differ.

HASSAN. And tomorrow?

DEBORAH. Don't bully me.

HASSAN. Please, humble request.

He waits, head slightly bowed, humbly supplicant.

DEBORAH (*flustered*). I shall sleep on it. (*She goes to the exit. He gazes at her.*)

HASSAN. Yes.

She tears herself from his glance and goes.

HASSAN (*mutters under his breath in Arabic*). This ewe camel escapes her hobbles.

The music changes to a sedate quickstep as HASSAN *dials out on a mobile telephone.*

HASSAN (*in Arabic*). The birds fly west.

MAN'S VOICE (*static, in Arabic*). Over the sea to the Islands.

HASSAN (*in Arabic*). Good – well?

MAN'S VOICE (*in Arabic*). Three Brigade certain, two and four on field manoeuvres and secure.

HASSAN (*in Arabic*). Where? Precise location?

MAN'S VOICE (*in Arabic*). Two hundred kilometres south west of the capital.

HASSAN (*in Arabic*). Three Brigade?

MAN'S VOICE (*in Arabic*). Moving against railways and telecommunications.

HASSAN (*in Arabic*). God be with you.

MAN'S VOICE (*in Arabic*). And with you, my Colonel.

HASSAN *pushes down the telephone aerial, laughs to himself.*

ALI (*approaches*). What? Yes . . . Three Brigade?

HASSAN. And Two and Four. (*They embrace.*)

ALI (*Arabic*). Allah be praised. (*English.*) Only fifty to one against us.

HASSAN. The odds will never be better.

ALI. These people from the oil company –

HASSAN (*quickly*). The woman is useful.

ALI. In what way, Colonel, in what way? (HASSAN *does not reply.*) I say get rid of them.

HASSAN. The good will of the Pedersen Oil Company is not unimportant to us.

ALI. Then remove the widow to safety, now.

HASSAN. No. I keep her.

ALI (*eager*). As hostage?

HASSAN. As honoured guest. The widow will focus attention – should we need it. (ALI *gives him an ironic look. They face each other.*)

ALI. Allah be with you.

HASSAN (*they clasp hands*). And with you, beloved and brave.

Act One, Scene Three

The terrace of the same house, the next morning. RHODA *is reading in a basket chair, whisky to hand.* STEPHANIE, *in riding breeches and pale silk shirt, enters as* RHODA *reaches down for her glass.*

STEPHANIE. Oh Gran, not this early! (*She groans, wincing.*)

RHODA. Medicinal. You sound as though you could do with a nip yourself.

STEPHANIE (*sits, lies back gratefully*). I fell off. Ohh, the air's marvellous here, your lungs feel like blue balloons. (*Sits up abruptly.*) You'll never guess! They gave me this cracking little Arab mare and she bucked me off . . . Brrmm, straight into the sand. I couldn't get my breath, and when I sat up and opened my eyes . . . guess what?

RHODA. You were being kissed by Errol Flynn.

STEPHANIE. What? Who's Errol Flynn?

RHODA. Oh never mind.

STEPHANIE (*shakes her head at the offer of* RHODA's *flask*).
No. I was lying in this valley, surrounded by stone columns!

RHODA. Ah! (*Of recognition.*) Lucky you didn't brain
yourself.

STEPHANIE. There were even some Corinthian capitals, just
lying about in the sand.

RHODA. I know the place. The Tuareg call it the Cleft.

STEPHANIE. We found some bits of pottery. David wanted to
pick them up but I wouldn't let him. He's got the most
amazing wrists.

RHODA. Huh!

STEPHANIE. Oh Gran, nobody's good enough for you.
Mummy says people who prefer plants to human beings
have something wrong with them.

RHODA. She's the expert.

STEPHANIE. Stop it. Where's Hassan?

RHODA. How should I know?

STEPHANIE *crosses to the drinks tray, refills* RHODA's
glass, and her silver flask. RHODA *grins.*

STEPHANIE. Tell me about him.

RHODA. Hassan . . . why?

STEPHANIE. I need to know. (RHODA *does not reply*.) You
trust me, don't you?

RHODA. Not entirely.

STEPHANIE (*after a pause*). I didn't realise that you had such
a poor opinion of me.

RHODA. My dear, you're rich.

STEPHANIE. I'm not to blame for that.

RHODA. Never met anyone rich who wasn't ruthless.

STEPHANIE. Oh you don't need to be rich for that. Take
Hassan.

RHODA. Ho ho ho! Fallen for him, have you? I should stick to your tennis player with the video camera . . . Whatshisname.

STEPHANIE. David? He's delicious, don't you think, well they all are. His relations. He's got hundreds . . . Oh, I adore families!

RHODA. I shouldn't put your faith in domesticity if I were you.

STEPHANIE. You did.

RHODA. No I didn't.

STEPHANIE. You had six children!

RHODA. Only by accident. Five stupid boys and your mother who made a mess of it.

STEPHANIE. She married Daddy, an important man!

RHODA. That's a matter of opinion. To give away your life! If there is such a thing as sin, that's it.

STEPHANIE. You mean because she gave up her work? I've never understood –

RHODA. He wouldn't have it.

STEPHANIE. Why not?

RHODA. Because your sainted father wanted a string of heirs for his global empire. A new Viking superbreed.

STEPHANIE. I see. (*Puzzled.*) Then why only me?

RHODA. I don't know. Low sperm count, I believe.

STEPHANIE. Oh. I hope it's not catching.

RHODA. You'll be all right.

STEPHANIE. Was she very famous?

RHODA. Your mother helped to break the code of life itself. And then abdicated. Walked away.

STEPHANIE. Why?!

RHODA. Because she's female – where's the lav, my bladder is about to explode.

STEPHANIE (*helps her up*). I don't think that's a good reason –

RHODA. Autres temps, my dear – thank God the bogs here aren't the squatting variety –

They go.

HASSAN *and* DEBORAH *enter. He is quoting poetry in Arabic. DEBORAH is looking very comely. He finishes.*

DEBORAH. Beautiful. (*He gestures at the coffee tray.*) Thank you.

HASSAN. You find it odd that a soldier should write poetry?

DEBORAH. Yes.

HASSAN. His only function is to kill – to destroy?

DEBORAH. Isn't that the case?

HASSAN. Sometimes. (*He brings her a cup of coffee.*) Unfortunately.

They stroll, and look out at the view.

HASSAN. Your daughter believes in submission as the answer to oppression.

DEBORAH. Indeed? You surprise me.

HASSAN. May I ask what you believe?

DEBORAH. Me? Oh don't ask me.

HASSAN. I do. I do ask you.

DEBORAH. I don't know. It depends.

HASSAN. On what? (*Suddenly urgent.*) On what?

DEBORAH. Colonel. Colonel, I know that this country is troubled. That there have been rumours of disaffection . . . an impending uprising. The Foreign Office were not at all keen for us to come.

HASSAN. Why did you come?

DEBORAH. Is it true?

HASSAN (*slight pause*). No. Who knows? A soldier must be prepared at all times.

DEBORAH. Even to kill his own countrymen?

HASSAN. The question of nationality may not be relevant. The decision to take life may not rest on this.

DEBORAH. You baffle me.

HASSAN. Ah yes! to you, no doubt, all life is sacrosanct. Yet you kill with every step. (*He bends, picks something up, shows it to her on the palm of his hand.*)

DEBORAH. Oh, it's only a beetle.

HASSAN. You don't find it beautiful? (*They inspect it, heads together.*) You will come to the mountains?

DEBORAH. Why is it important?

HASSAN. My house is empty. No-one walks in my garden. But you will. For you it will come to life. Please . . .

He falls on his knees before her. This arouses her compassion but she jerks up, horribly embarrassed, as ALI enters.

HASSAN (*rises imperturbably*). What is it?

ALI. Colonel, sir, report of disturbances.

HASSAN. Where?

ALI (*covering*). In the villages.

HASSAN. Let me see. (*They move apart. To DEBORAH.*) Excuse me. (*To ALI.*) Radio and communications?

ALI. Three Brigade. Confirmed.

HASSAN. Two Para?

ALI. In the city.

HASSAN (*smiles*). Now they all come. End of diversion, we must move to headquarters, now. (*Aloud.*) No, not important. Dispute over water. Continue as arranged, Captain.

ALI. Sir . . . Madame.

Salutes, goes, with a sharp look at them.

HASSAN (*rare smile*). Fate is on our side. Double reason to leave the area – to avoid small skirmish.

DEBORAH. Surely if there's trouble we should head for the coast?

HASSAN. Not necessary.

DEBORAH. But if there's likely to be –

HASSAN. Dear lady, for once in your life –

DEBORAH. Please Colonel –

HASSAN. My name is Hassan.

DEBORAH. What?

HASSAN. It is a dream. That you would call me by my name. Forgive me, I am too familiar.

DEBORAH. Yes I think you are.

HASSAN. I don't know what it is . . . you distract me . . . and I am a very busy man, I cannot afford this distraction.

DEBORAH *laughs, a lovely low laugh at his indignation. He smiles.*

HASSAN. Ah, I make you laugh! You are most lovely when you laugh, you must laugh often. Let me show you the route to the mountain . . . It's very beautiful . . .

He steers her off. A pause. RHODA *and* STEPHANIE *enter.*

STEPHANIE. Of course I like my own way, who doesn't, everybody does.

RHODA. You're spoilt.

STEPHANIE. You spoil me more than anybody.

RHODA. Of course, I'm your grandmother.

STEPHANIE. I want to be like you.

RHODA. What?

STEPHANIE. Nothing.

She settles RHODA into a basket chair, fetches another cushion, puts it behind RHODA's back. RHODA, who doesn't like the fuss, waves at her irritably.

STEPHANIE. All right?

RHODA. Of course I'm all right.

She squints up at STEPHANIE suspiciously.

STEPHANIE. Not too much sun?

RHODA scowls, then realises that STEPHANIE is teasing her.

RHODA (*growls*). Shan't leave you my Mesopotamian relics.

STEPHANIE. Oh good, you can read my Vogue.

RHODA pulls a face but takes it and turns the pages. STEPHANIE crosses to the ornate tray.

STEPHANIE. Coffee?

RHODA. Thanks. (*As STEPHANIE approaches with the coffee.*) With a chaser. (*Turns a page.*) I wish they'd design something for arthritic hands.

STEPHANIE. Your hands are beautiful.

RHODA (*to herself*). Bollocks. (*As ERIC enters, breathless.*) Eric, your hair's all the wrong way – what's up?

ERIC (*breathless*). Ah . . . ah . . . (*Dashes to the window and back.*)

RHODA. Are you coming or going?

ERIC (*breathless*). Good question. (*As STEPHANIE offers him coffee.*) Sorry, no time.

RHODA. Why, what's the matter. Something up? Not bad news? Spit it out, man.

ERIC. We may have to change our plans – yes, I will, please.

STEPHANIE *moves away to the coffee tray.*

RHODA. Why?

ERIC (*jerks his head at* STEPHANIE *behind her back. To* RHODA). Possible crisis. (RHODA *clicks, looks excited.*)

STEPHANIE. Why, what's happened? (*Brings coffee.*)

ERIC. I suggest that we get the hell out of here. Thanks.

RHODA (*aside*). Are you saying the balloon's gone up?

ERIC (*shrugs*). I can't get through to the capital.

RHODA. That's not unusual.

ERIC. I sent a boy down to the police station. There's no-one there and the streets are empty.

STEPHANIE *closes, alertly interested.*

RHODA. Mmm, sounds as though you're right. Lift-off, eh?

STEPHANIE (*excited*). What?

RHODA. Let's hope they haven't jumped the gun.

ERIC. Oh I think he's –

RHODA. Stephanie . . . (*She struggles out of her chair.*) It's up to the hills for us.

ERIC. No, no. Coast road for you ladies.

RHODA. Rubbish.

STEPHANIE *runs off.*

ERIC. All right, a helicopter –

RHODA. We'd better clear decks with Hassan. Stephanie – where's the girl gone now?

DEBORAH *enters.*

ERIC. Ah, Mrs. Pedersen. Look, no cause for alarm, but I was suggesting to Lady Wiggins that it might be advantageous to be on our way, so to speak.

DEBORAH. It's all been arranged.

ERIC. Oh, good.

DEBORAH. The Colonel will escort us.

RHODA. Up to the Rift?

ERIC. To the coast, I presume.

DEBORAH. No, no, we're taking a trip to the hills. He seems very keen –

ERIC. No, you mustn't do that.

RHODA. Why not? Topping idea.

ERIC. Ladies, please. I don't think you understand. This country could flare up at any moment. Mrs. Pedersen, I do apologise, most sincerely, but these things can happen very quickly and without warning –

DEBORAH. It's merely a local disturbance over water –

ERIC. I don't think –

DEBORAH. I remember when I was working here – these things blow over, isn't that so, Mother?

ERIC. Forgive me, I think this may be more than a local thing, I'd be much happier if you'd leave at once for the coast.

RHODA. Rubbish, they'll have blocked the road.

ERIC. You may well be right. Look, David's on the radio telephone, they'll have a boat waiting for us.

STEPHANIE (*enters*).What boat?

DAVID *enters separately.*

DAVID. It's OK, folks, there's a chopper on its way.

STEPHANIE. What?

RHODA. Whose?

DAVID. The company's –

STEPHANIE. No, no –

DAVID. Apparently there's been an attempted coup, one guy said there was an attack on the Palace!

RHODA. Did he now? (*She and* ERIC *exchange a look.*)

DAVID. Nobody seems to know what's going on, but they've advised us to get down to the coast, there's a launch waiting. (*To* STEPHANIE.) Everything's cool.

DEBORAH. Oh but . . . (*They wait for her to speak.*) But I don't . . . surely if . . .

STEPHANIE. Mummy, it's all right, honestly!

RHODA (*irritable with* DEBORAH). Oh God, girl . . .

DEBORAH. I was given assurances! I've agreed to . . . what is happening? (*To* ERIC.) You say one thing, he says another . . . I don't know who to believe!

RHODA. Well we don't need your hysterics for a start. You can push off to the coast if you want to risk everybody's life, you won't catch me, I'm going the other way, I know this territory.

DEBORAH. I was assured there was no risk! (HASSAN *enters.*) You said there was no risk!

ERIC. We must leave for the port now –

HASSAN. No.

DAVID. It's OK, there's a chopper on its way from the oilfields.

HASSAN. No. (*His sharpness arrests them.*) You cannot take it.

DAVID. Why not?

ERIC (*together*). Sorry, I must insist.

DEBORAH. You told me –

DAVID. That's why they're sending the transport, so that we –

HASSAN. You will be killed.

DEBORAH. What?!

ERIC. Look, Hassan –

HASSAN. Anti-aircraft is already in the hands of – insurgents.

DEBORAH. It's not a local disturbance? (*He shakes his head.*) But won't we be safe here, in a government residence?

RHODA. Hah!

ERIC. Oh I doubt that.

DEBORAH. But if our people, if the company advises –

HASSAN. I cannot allow it.

DEBORAH. Are you giving us orders?

HASSAN. For your safety, yes.

STEPHANIE. Mummy, do listen –

ERIC (*aside*). Hassan, I want these women out of here, now!

RHODA (*to* DEBORAH). Take my advice –

DEBORAH. That's the last thing I intend to do.

RHODA. If you're not careful you'll get us all killed!

HASSAN (*to* ERIC). Not possible, the coast road is under attack. (*Aloud.*) Madame, my men are waiting to escort you to safety.

RHODA. To Al Kaddur? (*She pronounces it the English way.*)

HASSAN. To Al Kaddur. . . in the mountains.

RHODA. It's no distance –

STEPHANIE. It's just a few hours, Mummy.

HASSAN. On the way pleasant oasis for cool drink, and then hills, with trees and many breezes –

DEBORAH (*distracted*). Yes, so you say –

DAVID. No look, I'm sorry, but I've just been on the link, they were absolutely adamant, that's why they're sending the helicopter, it's on the way. (HASSAN *leaves quickly.*) We can be in the port in twenty minutes.

ERIC. I have to stay, but you must all go, as quickly as possible.

RHODA. If we stick with Hassan we'll be all right.

STEPHANIE. Exactly!

DAVID. Mrs. Pedersen?

DEBORAH. I don't know, I don't know! I shouldn't be here, we should never have come!

The sound of a helicopter, gradually getting closer.

DAVID. I think I can hear it – we'd better get our stuff together –

RHODA. Not me, you won't catch me in an oil company chopper, seen them fall out of the skies too often. Deborah, I'm going with Hassan. If you've any sense you'll come with us – now where's my spongebag?

The helicopter, louder.

DAVID. That's it . . . (*He leaps about, looks up, waves.*) Great – that's great . . . bloody good! I say we leave the gear and make a run for it!

The others look out at the desert, shielding their eyes.

STEPHANIE. David, we can't!

RHODA. Young fool . . .

DAVID. They'll be here in a few minutes!

STEPHANIE. No!

DEBORAH. Darling?

STEPHANIE. We *must* stay with the army!

DEBORAH. Darling please! if you think I'll risk one hair of your head –

The noise of the helicopter.

DAVID. Come on!

ERIC. For God's sake –

HASSAN runs on swiftly.

HASSAN. Down, all of you – down!!

He grabs DEBORAH, *throws her down and covers her protectively. There is a burst of firing. The sound of the helicopter descending. An ominous change in the sound of its engine. The sound becomes very loud, followed by a very loud crump and a crash. A light flash as the helicopter bursts into flames.* STEPHANIE *screams. Silence.*

ERIC (*softly*). God help them.

DAVID *holds* STEPHANIE, *shielding her from the sight. She whimpers softly.*

RHODA. Oh my God.

DEBORAH *rises, stunned with shock.*

HASSAN. No! stay down.

He pulls her down and then runs off, crouched low.

DEBORAH. Why . . . why did I take a chance   why?

She whimpers, then is silent. A crackle of gunfire, close, then another, further away. And then silence. ERIC *rises.* DAVID *rises.* HASSAN *enters.*

HASSAN. Please. We must leave now.

ERIC. All right. As you say.

DEBORAH (*gabbles*). All I ask is her safety. Just protect her, that's all I ask.

RHODA. Deborah, shut up, now.

DAVID (*to* STEPHANIE). You OK?

STEPHANIE. Yes, thanks.

DEBORAH. Colonel, please, it's all I ask. My daughter's safety, that's all.

HASSAN. You should ask more, lady.

ERIC. Ready?

RHODA. Deborah?

STEPHANIE. Mummy?

DEBORAH *nods. The others straggle out. She and* HASSAN *follow them.*

HASSAN. You should ask more.

She looks at him and leaves. ALI *enters. He and* HASSAN *pause for a moment, exchanging a glance. They leave separately.*

Act Two, Scene One

The oasis. Palms, an open tent. ALI *preparing a meal in the background.* RHODA *and* ERIC *are lounging on cushions with glasses of mint tea.*

RHODA. Ali . . .

ALI. Madame?

RHODA. Put a tot in this for me, will you?

ALI *comes forward with the whisky bottle.* ERIC *lifts his glass too, and* DAVID *nods, offers his glass as* ALI *approaches.*

ERIC. Why not?

DAVID. Thanks. Very cold in the desert at night. Thanks Ali.

He drinks and prowls.

No sign of them. I suppose they *were* here.

ERIC. They'll be well ahead.

RHODA. Tucked up in Al Kaddur by now.

DAVID. Why did they have to whizz on so? No wonder we had a burn out.

RHODA. Relax – sit down. Did you get some good pictures of the oasis?

DAVID (*moody*). A few.

ERIC (*looking round*). Beautiful spot.

DAVID *grunts begrudging agreement.*

ERIC. One minute nothing but rock and shale, suddenly – palms and pomegranate trees . . .

RHODA. And big fat water melons. Top me up, Eric.

ERIC *rolls off his cushion, grabs the nearby bottle.* DAVID *drinks.*

DAVID. I don't like being separated. Gives me a sort of, I don't know, moody feeling. (*He sighs heavily.*) Like Beau Brummel.

ERIC (*calls*). Geste!

DAVID. Sorry?

RHODA. What?

ERIC. He means Beau Geste.

DAVID. Really? Well, either way I don't usually get protective with females. (*Sotto voce, to* RHODA.) They hate it.

RHODA. That a fact?

DAVID. One minute they like you with a rose in your teeth . . . next thing, you're accused of being patronising. I've never patronised anybody in my life – Ali, take these, there's a good chap. (*He gives* ALI *his cameras, reclines on the baggage.*)

ERIC. Marvellous smell, Ali.

RHODA *puts down her glass, lies back, stretching.*

RHODA. Mmmm . . . food!

DAVID. Funny how different you feel out here. I mean, take Steph. She's led a very protected life, had to get it all out of books, but she's tough, she knows what she wants.

RHODA. She's her father's daughter.

DAVID. Whereas Mrs. Pedersen, she's more what I'd call the traditional woman. She brings out the . . . ah . . . well, what I mean is, when women go independent, you don't feel so . . . so . . .

RHODA. Gallant?

DAVID. Absolutely. Then they call us shits.

ALI *sets down a large brass tray of food on a low wooden stand.*

RHODA. You're getting philosophical, have something to eat.

ERIC. Looks good, Ali, what have we got?

ALI (*pointing round the tray proudly*). Burning mutton, couscous, crushed tin strawberry with goaty curd – very fine! (DAVID *pulls a face.*)

DAVID. I think I'll stick to dates if you don't mind.

He sits apart on a boulder, eating and talking and spitting stones. RHODA *and* ERIC *help themselves to food.*

We were only supposed to be here two days, then off to Majorca for wind-surfing. More my style actually.

RHODA. David's in projects.

ERIC. What sort of projects?

DAVID. Anything, you name it – mustard, whale-meat, customised tours. Feasibility. We test the market.

ERIC (*chewing savagely*). The market!

RHODA. Now, Eric. Hah, I remember my husband smashing a boiled egg once because his shares had dived.

ERIC (*chuckles*). I told him – serves you right for gambling with people's lives, anyway, how can they be worth half overnight, the people are still there, the factories are there. He nearly did the same to my head.

DAVID. Ah, but you see, Lady Wiggins, nothing's worth anything. (ERIC *growls ominously.*) Not till you create a market for it.

ERIC (*mutters to himself*). Bloody young –

RHODA (*warning*). Eric!

ERIC *glares, gnaws on a mutton bone.*

Anyway, who are you to talk, you went commercial once. (*Jerks her head at* ERIC.) Suspended for knowing Anthony Blunt.

DAVID. Really?! Gosh, you could do a true-life – (*But* ERIC's *glare, as he chews savagely in the light of the fire, makes him trail off politely.*)

RHODA. He went into advertising. Not his finest hour.

ERIC. You loved it, you made up all my slogans. 'Lagonda, the Car of Tomorrow!'

RHODA. 'Drink Gin, Brings you On!' (DAVID *laughs*). We were all having a marvellous time on his expense account, free trips to Paris, Milan, and then you upped and chucked it!

ERIC. It was the barbecues.

DAVID. Sorry?

ERIC (*grinding his teeth*). House style, they called it. For the clients. They made us wear denim slacks.

RHODA. Jeans, you fool! you should have seen his face, above the open-necked shirt. (*Laughs dirtily.*) Gave all the company wives spontaneous abortions.

ERIC (*rears up in protest*). That was because you laced their milkshakes!

RHODA. Your recipe, dear heart . . .

ERIC (*mutters*). . . . . choke themselves . . .

RHODA. So you buzzed off to Africa to save your soul.

ERIC. No, no, it was the Italian boy.

RHODA. That little tease! Poor old Eric decides on heart of darkness as a cure and they send him to Kenya – to jip up the tourist industry.

DAVID (*interested*). Really?

ERIC. My brief was to persuade the tribes to make their carvings more primitive. The stuff they'd been doing for a thousand years was felt to be a bit Bambi.

DAVID. Sounds a good wheeze, did you crack it?

ERIC. Oh yes. We made the masks absolutely horrible. They sell for a fortune at Sothebys now.

DAVID. There you are, all a matter of the market. (*He leans forward and eats from the communal tray.*) I say, this sort of yellow mush isn't bad. (*He tucks in, head bent.*)

RHODA. Plenty to eat in the desert if you know where to look . . . locusts, bean beetle, stick-fly . . . (*Talking with her mouth full as she tucks in as well, leans to DAVID cordially.*) . . . There are some delicious white grubs in the sand if you poke about, they fry up like calves liver. Go on . . . (*Pushes the dish towards him.*)

DAVID. I don't think I will, if you don't mind.

RHODA *burps loudly.*

RHODA. That's better.

ALI *bends over* RHODA *with a tray.*

ALI. Coffee, madame?

RHODA. Oh, lovely – thick enough to walk on.

ERIC (*takes coffee*). Divine. (*He ladles in four sugars.*)

DAVID *lies back. He breathes deep.*

DAVID. Wow . . . the air's superb . . .

ERIC. Tastes of absolutely nothing.

RHODA. That's because of all the nothingness.

DAVID. God I could sleep.

He falls asleep almost as he speaks. ALI *takes his glass from him, puts a rolled jacket under his head, covers him lightly. He pours drinks for* ERIC *and* RHODA, *sees to the fire, and removes the tray and retires. Silence.* ERIC *and* RHODA *drink companionably before the fire.*

ERIC. I assume this is a set-up, our being left behind?

RHODA. I doubt it.

ERIC. You think it was genuine? Our breakdown? You'd better be right. If Hassan thinks he can use the Pedersens as –

RHODA. Come off it, Eric! No conspiracy theories, not at this time of night.

ERIC. The usual cock-up then?

RHODA. They call it the People Factor. That's what I read in the Daily Telegraph.

ERIC. Oh, do you read the Telegraph?

RHODA. Pass your glass.

They finish their drinks, settle down to sleep without ceremony. ALI intones his prayers. When they are motion-less he sets up his transmitter and begins to transmit.

Act Two, Scene Two

HASSAN *and* DEBORAH *in his garden at Al Kaddur.*

HASSAN. Be careful, the steps are wet.

DEBORAH. So many flowers . . . hibiscus, frangipani . . .

HASSAN. As you see, secret garden.

She slides down and sits, with her back against a tree, lifting her head, eyes closed, against the sun. For a moment he stands, looking down at her, then sits beside her.

HASSAN. You are comfortable?

DEBORAH (*lifting them with her hands*). Pine needles! Oh yes.

HASSAN. And you feel well?

DEBORAH. Very well.

She closes her eyes again. He looks at her profile.

HASSAN (*softly*). You wish for something.

DEBORAH (*eyes closed*). No. Nothing. (*Laughs gently.*)

HASSAN. What?

DEBORAH. I have everything, isn't that what you said?

HASSAN. Everything? No, I think not.

She opens her eyes, sits up, looks at him.

DEBORAH. You mean a lover, that's what you mean? Some fascinating creature to tell me witty jokes and –

HASSAN. And make love with you?

DEBORAH. Oh please.

HASSAN. I am sorry.

DEBORAH (*slight pause*). Colonel. Colonel, I have been recently widowed. As you know. Since you say that you, too, know loss and loneliness, then I can only leave you to deduce what I think of your cruel mockery. And I am less than charmed by your crude notions that I might be persuaded to whatever it is that you wish from me by your pathetic attempts at seduction. I was not, as they say, born yesterday.

HASSAN (*stoutly*). No, you were not.

DEBORAH. And what is that supposed to mean? And while we're on the subject, I have not been unaware of your furtive attempts to draw my daughter into private conversations –

HASSAN. You think too much of her.

DEBORAH. She's my daughter!

HASSAN. Who will soon leave you.

DEBORAH. In time, yes. She's still very young!

HASSAN. And you are old.

DEBORAH. Older. Not that old.

HASSAN. I think that you are in prison. (*Soft.*) And I, Hassan, seek to liberate.

DEBORAH. Liberate? (*Short laugh.*) Oh, I think you mean capture.

HASSAN. Yes. That as well. You are a very useful woman, although not at this moment.

DEBORAH. Oh?

HASSAN. At this moment you are deflecting me. (*He plays with her bare foot.*) I think you know that.

DEBORAH. I know that something's up . . . that there's something in the air . . . You'd be a fool not to feel it . . .

HASSAN. Please, don't worry, you are safe here. Mrs. Pedersen . . . You know what I feel for you. And I think . . . I know that you feel something for me.

Slight pause.

DEBORAH. All right. Perhaps. In that case – tell me the truth.

HASSAN. I desire you.

DEBORAH. Yes, yes, yes, I know that, so you keep saying. Now I'd like to know. All the way here in the car you said not a word to Stephanie, and she never looked at you once. Why? What is going on, I need to know!

HASSAN. Please. I risk lives.

He kisses her. After a second she drowns in his kisses.

DEBORAH. No . . . no . . .

He kisses her again, longer and deeper.

Please . . . You must know you can trust me.

He strokes her hair.

HASSAN. Why, because you are a middle-class English-woman?

DEBORAH. Honestly –

HASSAN. No, please, yes, of course I trust you, why do you think I love you, your body is not so amazing –

DEBORAH. Thank you.

HASSAN. But good enough. What I love is your soul. Your soul is like the most beautiful flower . . . shining . . . fertile . . . capable of turning the whole world into a garden. Yet it is half alive. You have been dying a long while. Now – time to come alive. To open. To be useful.

Silence.

DEBORAH. Are we your hostages?

Silence. She gets up.

If you are playing for this country, Colonel Sa'id, then you need the good will of Pedersen Oil.

HASSAN. No. What I wish is *your* good will. Personal.

DEBORAH (*drily*). Why, what's that got to do with it?

HASSAN. Everything.

DEBORAH. Why?

HASSAN. Because, in the end, everything is personal. And because . . . I don't know why . . . When I am with you the maggots leave my head.

DEBORAH. Thank you, that's very flattering.

HASSAN. And of course I desire you. You are a sweet herb, a branch of fragrant rosemary, swaying in the wind on a hillside, a . . . (*But he is tired.*)

DEBORAH. Garlic bulb?

He laughs and pulls her down beside him.

HASSAN. I am so sorry. There is no time.

He kisses her. As the kiss deepens there is the sound of a car hooting urgently. He does not hear it. It hoots again. He rolls off her.

DEBORAH. What is it?

HASSAN. I must leave you. Wait. Wait for me. All will be well. Wait.

He goes quickly. DEBORAH *sits up, dazed by his embrace.
The sound of a car, driving off at speed. The sound merges,
becomes the sound of a car being revved and tested.*

RHODA, *at the oasis, heaves and puffs, putting the baggage
together in a practised way. The tent has been struck.*
DAVID *lunges on.*

DAVID. Ali's got it going!

RHODA. So I hear.

DAVID. Sorry, am I in your way?

RHODA. Could you roll up the carpet?

DAVID. What? Oh – right. (*As* RHODA *staggers with a
bundle.*) Here, let me take that. (*But as she does he sinks to
the ground with it.*) Wow! you must be strong.

RHODA (*rolling rugs, jerks her head at a pile already rolled*).
And the rugs.

DAVID *heaves the bundle off, comes straight back, attempts
to pick up the rugs. They are long and bendy and defeat him.*

DAVID. Sure. (*He puffs, tackling the rugs, stops for a rest,
with one foot on the rugs like a game hunter.*) I work out
quite a bit, you know.

RHODA, *busy, gives him a sardonic look.*

I went on this course where you have to treat your body as a
temple. (*He gets the rugs up, swings, and fells* ERIC.) Oh,
sorry.

ERIC. Allow me. (*He takes the rugs and goes.*)

DAVID. Right. (*He watches* RHODA *work.*) No, as I was
saying, Lady Wiggins, I don't want to be some big wheel or
anything, I mean, like, feature . . . In fact I could do without
most things, well except money of course. (*A clatter as he
knocks the cans over.*)

ERIC. Careful! (*He takes the thread of cans and marches off.*)

DAVID. Sorry! (*To* RHODA.) Need any help?

She gives him an eloquent look, shakes her head firmly. He sits on the baggage.

What I really want is to *add* something to the world. (RHODA *reels off with a pile of baggage, returns at once.*) Contribute.

RHODA (*gasps, picking up the last bundle*). What did you have in mind? (*She totters off and comes straight back.*)

DAVID. Actually . . . between ourselves . . . I've got a lot of time for Mother Theresa.

RHODA (*drily*). You want to be a nun?

DAVID (*laughs*). No, you know. (RHODA *sinks down, weary.*) The trouble is I'm not ambitious. Not like my father. He said he only took his peerage for my mother's sake – she'd left him for Nina, the ballerina, yonks before that. I really hate all this – you know, insincerity. Like Christmas. I never give presents.

RHODA. You don't believe in religion?

DAVID. God no. (*He looks across at* RHODA, *wilting in the morning light.*) You're lucky. (*She's too pooped even to raise her head.*) With all this ecology lark – save the trees. It must be great having a cause. (*He sighs heavily.*) It could happen to me, I suppose. I could suddenly get up . . . (*He leaps up, knocking things over.*) . . . turn round, get a burning flash like Saint Peter on the road to Cairo.

ERIC (*enters with a map*). Saint Paul. Damascus.

DAVID. Sorry? Ah! (*He looms over* ERIC's *shoulder eagerly.*)

ERIC. We're here. Al Kaddur . . . I'd say about . . .

DAVID. Forty – fifty kilometres –

ERIC. Give or take –

A piercing scream rends the air.

RHODA. Oh bugger. (ERIC *runs off. He and* ALI *return supporting* DEBORAH. ALI *shouts to her driver in Arabic that all is well.*) David, the camp chair – quick.

DAVID *has trouble setting it up, manages it at last.*

ERIC. Here sit down, Mrs. Pedersen.

RHODA. What's up, are you hurt? Ali – (ALI *nods and goes.*)

DAVID *throws a cushion from* RHODA'*s last pile.* ERIC
fields it, slips it behind DEBORAH'*s back as* ALI *runs back
on.* RHODA *whispers to him, he nods and goes.*

DEBORAH Please . . . !

DAVID *runs off quickly.*

RHODA. What was all that noise about?

DEBORAH. I didn't know it was you, how did I know it was
you – please, you must ring the oil fields –

DAVID (*comes back quickly*). Where's Stephanie?

DEBORAH. The Captain . . . we must organise . . . the army,
set up a search –

DAVID. Isn't she with you?

ERIC. Where's the Colonel?

RHODA (*together*). Is she with Hassan?

DEBORAH (*howls*). Yes!!

RHODA. Oh, good.

DEBORAH. No!! I ran after them, I hung on to the car door . . .
I wouldn't let go – look! (*She shows them her knees,
adorned with neat pink plasters.*)

RHODA (*shouts*). Ali, bring the – oh. (*As* ALI *runs on with a
tray and pours tea into a glass with rapid dexterity.*)

ERIC. Please. Try not to cry. Tell me everything, it's important.

DEBORAH. Where were you?

ERIC. A breakdown –

DAVID. It's taken all night to fix the engine –

ALI. Tea, Madame.

RHODA. Go on, drink it.

DEBORAH. It's hot!

RHODA. Get it down, girl.

DEBORAH. How can you sit there?

DAVID. Where did they go?

ERIC. Did he take her – I mean –

RHODA. You said she was with –

DEBORAH. She was at the wheel – she was driving!

They gaze at her, baffled. Even ALI *frowns.*

ERIC (*gently*). Mrs. Pedersen . . . Mrs. Pedersen. I want you to tell me what happened. From the beginning. (*His voice soothes her. She takes the tea obediently and sips.*) You were in the car ahead of us, with your daughter and the Colonel . . .

DEBORAH (*snarls*). All squashed together with those great thighs stuck between us . . . wretched car with no air-conditioning – you *had* to have the windows open!

DAVID. Sorry?

DEBORAH. The scent – the scent!

DAVID. He wasn't wearing scent! (*Shocked.*)

DEBORAH. Who?

DAVID. Well –

DEBORAH. The orange blossom! From the trees!

RHODA. Oh, you mean up the mountain? That's old Wendy's work! I helped her plant them all the way to the Rift.

DEBORAH. I should have seen it –

RHODA. Supposed to be for the people –

DEBORAH. I should have known –

DAVID. Known what?

RHODA. – of course the poor buggers daren't lay a finger on the oranges –

ERIC. But you arrived safely –

RHODA. – bloody police cop the lot.

DEBORAH. Mother will you please stop swearing, you sound like a   (*She searches for a word.*) . . . Like a hippy!

This makes DAVID laugh.

ERIC. You arrived at Al Kaddur?

DEBORAH. Yes!

ERIC. And? What was happening? Who was there?

DEBORAH. Soldiers! – thousands of them – guns, armoured trucks –

ERIC. How many? How many?

DEBORAH. How should I know!

ERIC. What were they doing?

DEBORAH. Playing boule, most of them, on the –

DAVID. Boule?

DEBORAH. It's a sort of game – ohh! – please!

RHODA. Here . . . (*Brandishes her hip flask.*) Let me put something in it for you.

DEBORAH *sips her laced tea. They wait for her to go on.*

DEBORAH. They sat us down, at a table.

ERIC (*prompts her as she falters*). In the house?

DEBORAH (*irritable*). No, in the garden! (*Sighs patiently at the interruption*). There were drinks . . . Sherbet, fresh lemon for Stephanie . . .

RHODA. Well that was civil.

DEBORAH. He insisted on showing me the flowers!

She fidgets, looking in her bag for her handkerchief. ERIC takes out a large white one, but she ignores him, head down, finds a handkerchief with a wide border of lace, wipes her eyes.

RHODA. Where was Stephanie?

DEBORAH (*wails*). I don't know! I left her . . . on the terrace!

RHODA. You went off with Hassan – on your own?

DEBORAH. Only to divert his attention!

ERIC. Why?

RHODA. Who? What from? Stephanie? (*She bursts out laughing.*)

DEBORAH. It's her first time away from the farm! She's impressionable!

RHODA. That's rich. I see. (*Laughs.*) Sounds as if you gave old Hassan the wrong idea – oh do stop snivelling.

DAVID *puts an arm about* DEBORAH's *shoulders.*

DAVID. I think you're marvellous.

RHODA. What are you getting so upset about? (*She puts a cigarette into a long amber holder,* ALI *gives her a light.*) Thanks. What happened – anything?

ERIC. Rhoda –

DAVID. Let's leave it, shall we?

RHODA. You were in the garden with Hassan . . . (*She cackles to herself.* DEBORAH *weeps quietly.*) Well?

DEBORAH. I . . . (*Dry sob.*) I . . .

RHODA. Go on, spit it out. You might as well!

DEBORAH. I wanted . . .

She cries.

All my life I –

Why?!

You give, give, give, give, give . . .

Why not? I thought it was natural to be generous . . .

That everybody . . .

She breaks off, flat.

Oh, what's the point?

RHODA (*grabs* ERIC's *large handkerchief*). Here, blow your nose.

DEBORAH *blows her nose loudly, sniffs.*

You always were a chump. Drink your tea and forget it, that's my advice.

DEBORAH. Why did I do it?

RHODA. I know these chaps. Forget the garden, whatever happened, best forgotten.

DEBORAH. Happened, what do you mean, happened? (*Snarls, out of control.*) NOTHING happened!!

Silence.

RHODA. Well if nothing happened –

DEBORAH. He said he's come back!

Silence. She sniffs miserably.

RHODA. Then what? He left you in the garden, what happened *then*?

DEBORAH (*small voice*). I waited.

RHODA. And? (DEBORAH *does not reply.*) And?

DEBORAH. Nothing.

RHODA. Nothing? (ERIC *whispers apart to* ALI.)

DEBORAH. Nothing at all. I sat under this enormous incense tree (*She snivels quietly to herself, wipes her nose on the lace-edged handkerchief.*)

RHODA. And then?

DEBORAH. A servant came out with a plate of iced cakes.

RHODA *laughs.*

DAVID. But – where did he go, did he say?

DEBORAH. Of course not, it was a trick, don't you see? I knew! I got up, sent the cakes flying, I couldn't find the way, it was a labyrinth, I had to go back and start again, when I got to the wall I leaned over and they saw me –

RHODA. Who?

DEBORAH. Stephanie – and him! I ran down as fast as I could, I held on to the –

RHODA. Yes, yes, yes – (*As* DEBORAH *rips off a plaster.*) It's only a graze –

DAVID. Are you saying Stephanie's been kidnapped?

ERIC. But surely, if she was driving –

DEBORAH. It's a trick – they tricked her! We must get in touch with the Palace, we'll agree to anything, we'll pay anything . . . Please, you must understand, I can't bear it . . . I'm responsible! He's a liar.

ERIC (*nods to* ALI). We must get on to Al Kaddur.

DEBORAH. No!

RHODA. They let *you* go, they gave you a car and driver –

DEBORAH (*snarls*). To get the money . . . I said I'd get the money!

RHODA. Rubbish, sit down and stop dribbling.

DAVID. Lady Wiggins, perhaps we should –

RHODA. Have some sense. If they drove off like that it was because they wanted to be on their own.

DEBORAH. Why? what for?

RHODA. How the hell should I know? (*Cackles.*) Perhaps they're in love.

DAVID. What?

DEBORAH. What did you say?

RHODA. You heard me.

DEBORAH *slaps her mother's face.*

RHODA. Ow! Do that again and I'll slap you back. Now that's enough, Deborah.

DEBORAH. How dare you utter such filth, you vicious interfering old –

RHODA. Don't you –

DAVID. Please, Mrs. Pedersen's upset!

RHODA. What do you think the girl's doing – it's desperation! Cooped up in that farmhouse being educated by post – at least your father and I took you all about with us.

DEBORAH. We weren't the children of Per Pedersen! – anyway, your way was eccentric . . . sloppy.

RHODA. So's life.

DEBORAH. You've never understood. Running around the edge planting a few trees, where is that going to get us? it's science that's changing the world –

RHODA. Yes, and not for the better!

DEBORAH. My husband brought more benefits, more happiness to more people –

The whine of a rifle shot.

ERIC. Down, everybody – quick!

Further gun fire.

Ali, the guns. Get down!

DEBORAH. What?

RHODA. Down, you fool!

DAVID. What's going on? (*As* ALI *hands him a gun.*) What do I do?

ERIC. See him – shooting at us?

They duck as a bullet whines.

DAVID. But they're government troops . . . they're on our side!

DEBORAH rises, grabs DAVID's gun from him, throws it aside. She approaches.

DEBORAH (*in Arabic*).Cease fire, beloved brothers, lest you harm those who love you and gave you birth. In the name of Allah. (*In English.*) Stop it at once – all of you!

The rifle fire stops. Silence.

ERIC. Good God.

RHODA. I'll be damned!

Act Two, Scene Three

The inner court of HASSAN 's house at Al Kaddur. Simple Moorish architecture. Birdsong. DEBORAH is walking up and down, her manner agitated. ERIC enters. She wheels, but he shakes his head apologetically as DAVID enters.

DEBORAH. Anything?

DAVID. Not as yet, no. Are you all right?

DEBORAH. No of course I'm not all right.

He hovers round her as if she is the Virgin Mary.

What is it?

DAVID. I can't . . . I mean – the way you . . . (*He shakes his head in wonder.*) I'll never forget it. You're a heroine, Mrs. Pedersen.

DEBORAH. No, I'm not, it was totally hysterical, and don't you ever, ever be so foolish as to –

DAVID. One look at you and they all put down their guns. You must have an amazing power –

DEBORAH. Yes, money! I was carrying travellers' cheques, why else do you think they co-operated?

ERIC. David, see if you can rustle up some breakfast, will you? Just coffee, croissants –

DAVID. Sure thing.

He rushes off. A pause.

ERIC. I did speak to the Adjutant.

DEBORAH *pauses in her pacing, approaches* ERIC.

DEBORAH. Mr. Bellairs –

ERIC. Oh do call me Eric. (*Silence. She walks. Then stops.*)

DEBORAH. Mr. Bellairs, I was wondering – how are Don and Cynthia these days?

ERIC. I beg your pardon?

DEBORAH. The Smith-Hendersons. You must know them awfully well. And little Hayley, from the overseas office, how is she? You heard about her accident?

ERIC. Afraid not.

DEBORAH. Who's in charge of P.R. now?

ERIC. P.R.?

DEBORAH. At the British Council.

Silence.

ERIC. I'm not on the staff, so to speak.

DEBORAH. I see.

ERIC. More of a co-optee.

DEBORAH. On an ad hoc basis, no doubt.

ERIC. Precisely.

DEBORAH. Oh please! (*Pause.*) What did you say to them?

ERIC. I beg your pardon?

DEBORAH. Out there. In the desert. After I did my best to get us all killed. You talked to them, the soldiers, you and the Captain. Then my mother started up in her appalling Arabic – what were you talking about?

ERIC. Merely asking for their help . . . as guests in their country.

DEBORAH. So they escorted us here. To Al Kaddur.

ERIC. Yes, that's right.

DEBORAH. You drove ahead. And when *we* arrived they were being marched off, the government troops, at gunpoint.

ERIC. Ah, no, it's . . . ah . . . they're . . . well, not now.

DEBORAH. I can see that. They are all out there, stripped down to their singlets, playing football with the rest of the rebels.

You must think I'm a fool. You're not British Council. Who are you? By whose authority are you empowered to risk the lives of British subjects?

ERIC. I am acting as liaison –

DEBORAH. I want to know.

ERIC. You must understand my position –

DEBORAH. On what basis? On the basis of a tissue of lies? Find her!! Whatever is going on here – I'm not a fool . . . Everything must be put aside – tell them anything, promise whatever you must . . . Change sides if necessary – look, I know the history of this country, I'm not unaware of –

ERIC. She's in no danger. We're out of radio contact at the moment but you must believe me . . . The situation is confused, but not dangerous.

DEBORAH. Tell me!

RHODA (*puts her head round an armchair*). He can't. It's known as 'need to know'.

DEBORAH. Oh for God's sake!

ERIC. I guarantee –

DEBORAH. That's not enough! If I must I'll drive out into the desert myself, in fact, if you would be good enough to order me a car –

In the distance, the rumble of heavy guns.

RHODA. Hullo!

ERIC. Honestly, that would be most unwise.

RHODA. If I were you –

DEBORAH. Go away! Where is she? I'm going mad, I feel totally unreal, it's as though life itself has stopped, as though –

ERIC. We're doing our best –

DAVID (*wheeling on with a breakfast tray*). Here we are – I'm ravenous – (*As* ERIC *wheels him off firmly.*) But you said –

ERIC. Not just now. (*He goes as well.*)

DEBORAH *stares after them helplessly, then resumes her restless pacing.*

RHODA. Oh do sit down, you're getting on my nerves.

DEBORAH. I have nothing to say to you.

RHODA. Suit yourself.

DEBORAH. Sitting there with a smug look on your face – all right, if you know it all, tell me!

RHODA. Oh no.

DEBORAH. Why not?

RHODA. Because you don't wish to hear.

DEBORAH. You've always been jealous because Stephanie and I are so close. And not a good word for Per though you took enough money off him for your silly schemes. I shall never believe she went of her own free will – never!

RHODA (*slight pause*). They met in London. In your company office. During the talks.

DEBORAH. Rubbish, she would have told me.

RHODA. Whose idea was it to come out here?

DEBORAH. The company's. I agreed to it.

RHODA. You agreed to the donation, not to hand it over in person. It's not your style, you hate travelling.

DEBORAH. Stephanie had just finished her exams, she needed a break.

RHODA. Stephanie is her father's daughter.

DEBORAH. We had a personal invitation from the King! After we endowed the new hospital

RHODA. Private clinic for his offspring, you mean, they run into hundreds.

DEBORAH. Mother please don't exaggerate.

RHODA. Father of the People? This country is a police state, it runs on terror – ask Hassan . . . (As HASSAN enters.) . . . He's been freedom fighting for years, ever since he was at LSE and lodged in my attic.

HASSAN. Good morning –

DEBORAH. Where is she? What have you done with her? Is she alive . . . please . . . please!

HASSAN. I'm sorry?

DEBORAH. My daughter!

HASSAN. I am very busy just now –

DEBORAH. I'll pay anything – anything –

RHODA (to HASSAN as he tries to evade DEBORAH). Well?

HASSAN. It is done.

RHODA (quietly). Thank God.

DEBORAH. Where is she, is she – ?

RHODA. Casualties?

HASSAN. Not many. As we expected. The Palace is burned.

STEPHANIE *runs on, embraces* DEBORAH *briefly, then hugs* RHODA.

STEPHANIE. Mummy . . . Gran, isn't it wonderful?

DEBORAH. Oh!! Oh, you're safe . . . ohhh . . .

STEPHANIE. What's the matter?

DEBORAH. You're here! What happened, where were you?

STEPHANIE. In the lav, I was feeling a bit queasy –

DEBORAH. No, before – didn't you see me? You must have seen me, you were driving –

STEPHANIE. Oh that – darling, I'm so sorry, we couldn't stop – emergency.

DAVID (*not seeing* STEPHANIE). All right, Colonel – where is she? (*He makes to attack* HASSAN *who fells him with a casual blow*.)

STEPHANIE. David!

Act Two, Scene Four

HASSAN'*s house, later. The sounds of celebration and cheering.* DEBORAH *enters, and sits, alone.* DAVID *enters, moves towards her, thinks better of it, moves away.* ERIC *enters with* STEPHANIE, *followed by* HASSAN *and* ALI.

ERIC. – I remember we had fireworks in Kuala Lumpur . . .

STEPHANIE. Such fun . . . and so many people!

ALI. Bravo, magnifique!

HASSAN (*to* ALI). Well?

ALI. The roads are clear, the mines have been removed.

RHODA *enters in ceremonial djellabah.*

RHODA. Ready?

DEBORAH. Oh, Mother! Ready for what?

ERIC. Triumphal trip to the capital?

RHODA. I'm game – safe, I presume?

HASSAN. Absolutely.

ALI. We guarantee. Full escort, but not necessary.

RHODA. Give me ten minutes. Deborah?

ERIC. Mrs. Pedersen?

STEPHANIE. Mummy?

Silence.

DEBORAH. You knew. All of you. Even my own mother –

RHODA. Now don't start –

DEBORAH. Am I so unimportant? Yes of course. Who am I?
    A private citizen.

HASSAN. Please –

DEBORAH. I count for nothing, with any of you, and shall I
    tell you why? Because I haven't sought power. I haven't
    wished to dominate – therefore I must be nothing.

RHODA. Rubbish.

DEBORAH. Even you. . . my own daughter. Losing your father
    was pain, but this is worse.

RHODA. Deborah, you're making a fool of yourself.

DEBORAH. Oh yes. Oh yes. I do beg all your pardons. I'll
    remove myself and leave you all to more vital matters, such
    as whom to imprison. I have cancelled the cheque.

STEPHANIE. Mother!

ERIC. The river money?

RHODA. That is not acceptable.

HASSAN (*lifts a hand*). It makes no difference. We shall take
    the oil fields. They belong to us.

DEBORAH. As I say, I have no gun. But this country is deeply in debt. To foreign banks – with whom we have established and fruitful relationships.

HASSAN (*slaps his thigh, making* DEBORAH *jump*). Good! You see? You fight! Good, Mrs. Pedersen. But we shall win.

DEBORAH. We'll find out – in the international courts.

She goes.

STEPHANIE. Mummy, please!

She follows DEBORAH *off.* HASSAN *moves swiftly, follows them.*

RHODA (*slight pause*). Well, Eric, when people make a mess of things, they're determined to see chaos all round. I'd better go and umpire. (*She goes.*)

ERIC (*calls after her*). Are you sure that's wise?

He and ALI *laugh.*

Oh dear. Ali, old friend, all packed up here?

ALI. All done. Communication dismantled – everything ready to go.

ERIC. I'll get my chaps and equipment out of your way. You for the treasury? (*They share a roll-up.*)

ALI. I would prefer Board of Trade. Has Hassan Sa'id ibn Sa'id spoken to you?

ERIC (*alert*). About what?

ALI. He hopes that you may be able to join us. Advisory capacity. You know the country, the people –

ERIC. Wish it were in my power.

ALI. We can make you very good, interesting post.

ERIC. Sorry, not in my hands, Ali.

ALI. Perhaps we make word with your government.

ERIC. Oh, I'm not government – God forbid!

ALI. Oh?

ERIC. No, no. Civil Service. Different cup of tea altogether.

ALI (*drily*). Cricket rather than soccer?

ERIC. Absolutely.

ALI. Please stay.

ERIC. Nothing I'd like better. It's back to a cold wet country for me, I'm dreading the winters.

ALI. Why go?

ERIC. I'm English.

ALI (*laughs quietly*). Where we are born is who we are. We shall miss you. (*They clasp hands.*)

ERIC. This is a most beautiful country.

ALI (*depressed*). Pray Allah we don't despoil. (*He goes.*)

ERIC. Amen to that. (*He goes separately.*)

Act Two, Scene Five

HASSAN's *office in the capital. A window open onto blue sky, white buildings, and the minaret of a mosque.* HASSAN *is working at his desk. He looks up as* ALI *enters.*

ALI. Lady Wiggins is here, Chief Minister. (*He goes.*)

HASSAN. Yes. Good. (*He gets up as* RHODA *enters.*)

RHODA. Hassan! So here you are. Not a very big office.

HASSAN. Not a very big country, beloved Umm. (*He gives her a drink.*)

RHODA. Fifteen million, the right size. Same with towns and villages . . . Too small, cankered, too big, mindless . . . Must get the size right, eh? (*She sniggers. He smiles at her fondly.*) Hurry up.

HASSAN. I am sorry?

RHODA. We're all waiting for you. (*He looks blank.*) The agricultural symposium. (HASSAN *groans.*) No need to stay, just look in again at five for the plenary session. Here's your speech – and do please stress the last para . . . The overgrazing's got to stop . . . Beans, we must grow beans. (*She shoves him out. He goes reluctantly.*) And avoid the Professor from Armenia, his crop results are fake. Stress beans

HASSAN *reaches back, takes a wad of paper from his desk, thrusts it at her.*

HASSAN. Rotation plans.

Grins as RHODA, *laden with paper, groans. She flops down at his desk, looks at the paper with disfavour. Turns over pages, shakes her head, settles down to read and make notes. A knock.* RHODA *looks up.*

RHODA. Oh, it's you.

DEBORAH *enters. She is wearing a linen suit, wears a hat, carries a bag and a small valise.*

I take it you're leaving?

DEBORAH. You might tell me where I can find Stephanie.

RHODA. No idea – somewhere in this warren.

DEBORAH. I need to know how long she intends to stay. (RHODA *does not reply.*) Do you know?

RHODA. I'm not her boss.

DEBORAH. Mother, she is just seventeen! Apart from anything else I shall have to make financial arrangements for her.

RHODA. She'll stay as long as he stays, I suppose.

DEBORAH. It's an adolescent crush! It won't last five minutes.

RHODA. Oh I think it's gone further than that.

DEBORAH. You'd know, of course, but then, you know everything.

RHODA (*chortles*). I know enough to know she's pregnant.

Silence.

DEBORAH. What did you say?

RHODA. I thought that would send you cross-eyed.

DEBORAH. If you weren't her grandmother I'd sue you for slander. Did Stephanie tell you? – no, of course not, because it isn't

RHODA. I don't need to be told –

DEBORAH. I see. Divination, was it?

RHODA. No, puke. I can still smell, and if you weren't so bloody out of touch with the world . . . (*As* STEPHANIE *enters.*) . . . Ah, there you are. Your mother wants to say goodbye.

STEPHANIE. Hullo, Mother.

RHODA (*to* DEBORAH). Well?

DEBORAH. Yes. I'm leaving, the car's waiting.

STEPHANIE. I didn't think you'd go.

DEBORAH. I've made some temporary arrangements for you. Here, it's all in the folder. Don't forget to sign the backs of the cards.

STEPHANIE. Please don't! Mum . . . it's so small. Cancelling the donation . . . they need it!

RHODA. That's the way she's always been.

STEPHANIE. No, it isn't. (*To* DEBORAH.) I've seen you upset. Never small.

DEBORAH *gives her an agonised look, picks up her case.*

What are you going to do?

DEBORAH. I'm going home!

STEPHANIE. I mean, when you get there?

DEBORAH. What I've always done – work.

STEPHANIE. The farm runs itself. You were saying last winter how bored you were.

DEBORAH. And what about University?

STEPHANIE. Who cares about University? This is Life!

RHODA. Absolutely!

DEBORAH. Mother! (*To* STEPHANIE.) They want to make use of you.

STEPHANIE. I know. Isn't it wonderful?

DEBORAH. You'll be exploited, they'll try to manipulate you for their own – well, they're wasting their time. Everything is in trust, you have no power of action.

STEPHANIE. Don't be too sure of that. Gran's right. I'm rich, therefore I'm ruthless . . . right, Gran? (RHODA *laughs*.) If I want money . . . (*She sighs deeply.*) I honestly thought you were different. You wouldn't compete, climb on people's faces. I thought you were above all that. Don't tell me it was just good old English meanness.

DEBORAH. Please come home.

STEPHANIE. I'm sorry. I can't. I'm pregnant.

DEBORAH. Oh, Steph – (*She covers her mouth, eyes wide.*)

STEPHANIE. Were *you* sick all the time? I'm sick *all* the time . . . All day, every day. I threw up on the path just now! The wind blew it back in my hair, I didn't even have a Kleenex, I had to use my knickers.

DEBORAH. It's his child?

STEPHANIE. It would be so nice if you stayed.

DEBORAH'*s knees give way. She sits, clasping her bag.*

DEBORAH. Have you told him, does he know?

STEPHANIE. Yes.

DEBORAH. You don't belong here!

STEPHANIE. Please stay.

DEBORAH. I can't. I have business in London – besides, the heat.

STEPHANIE. You spent three hours in the sun with those children yesterday – without even a hat.

DEBORAH. We don't belong. It's their country. They've fought for it, let them have it. Stephanie not like this, in this place. A child needs security, stability – believe me, I know!

RHODA. You had a perfectly secure childhood,

DEBORAH. Rubbish, you never took your hat off. All those causes that were so much more important than we were – as for Daddy –

RHODA. Oh, that fool.

DEBORAH. As you never tired of telling him, I don't know why he didn't shove your face in the appalling grub you put in front of us –

RHODA. You had everything . . . books, travel –

DEBORAH. We *bored* you! I tried everything, being good, winning scholarships. The boys gave up . . . They're weaker, you see, they can't do without it.

STEPHANIE. Do without what ?

DEBORAH. Love. But we can, can't we, Mother?

RHODA. I don't know what you're talking about.

HASSAN *enters.*

For God's sake, you can't hang on to the girl forever . . .

HASSAN. Mesdames . . .

RHODA. Tell her, Hassan!

HASSAN. Please?

DEBORAH. Oh you think you've got it right, you clever people who want to tell us how to live. Until it ends in war

and chaos and you decamp with your Swiss bank accounts.
Where have you brought us, tell me that?

HASSAN. What is the matter?

DEBORAH. Oh, nothing of importance. The fact that you have
assaulted my daughter, that you have invaded –

STEPHANIE. Ooergh, quick – bathroom?

RHODA. Blue door on the right.

    STEPHANIE *dashes out.*

DEBORAH. Darling! (*She turns on* HASSAN.) It's not as
though you could make her happy.

HASSAN. Happy? Is this relevant?

DEBORAH. Shut up – you may think, Colonel Sa'id, that you
can mislead an old woman and a girl, but I am not the fool
you take me for.

RHODA. Ha ha!

HASSAN. Indeed you are not –

DEBORAH. I'm glad you agree. My husband, at all times, kept
me fully informed. I have not been unaware of connections
between Pedersen Oil and certain active elements here. Our
attitude, as you know, has been cordial. I'm surprised that
you should wish to jeopardise relationships with those who
may have your interests at heart.

RHODA. She's trying to buy you off, Hassan.

DEBORAH. Oh yes, it's all about Buying, is it not, Colonel?
Buying is what it's all about, so may I remind you of the
outstanding interest on our loans to your Treasury, for which
your government is legally liable.

HASSAN. That is arguable.

DEBORAH. Argument, Colonel Sa'id, costs money. Of course,
it is possible that the payments might be waived, even the
principle in part –

HASSAN. This has already been suggested to us.

DEBORAH. Without my signature, worthless.

RHODA. Deborah, if you start mucking about with that devilish consortium of your husband's they'll declare you bonkers and shove you inside.

DEBORAH (*snarls*). I can buy all the psychiatrists I need, thank you very much. My companies and I are not supplicants, Colonel. Who undertook the original development here? Imported the skills? Took the risk?

HASSAN (*smoothly*). On whose behalf? Ours? Millions of dollars disappear daily on the magic carpets of your so highly-paid accountants. Prices are decided not by us, but by you, for your convenience.

DEBORAH. There is nothing that cannot be changed.

HASSAN. You are right. But who are we against multi-nationals? Mere feathers in the wind. (*Slight pause.*) Your offer, please.

DEBORAH. Co-partnership.

HASSAN. Co-partnership?

DEBORAH. Forty-nine, fifty-one. To us. In order to guarantee production. (HASSAN *looks at her heavily.*) Something of an increase on your present ten per cent.

HASSAN. Most generous. And the consideration?

DEBORAH. I'm sorry?

HASSAN. What do you want? In return?

DEBORAH. My daughter.

HASSAN (*prompt*). Have her.

STEPHANIE *enters, slightly wan from being sick again.*

DEBORAH. Darling, are you all right?

STEPHANIE. Yes, thank you.

DEBORAH. And you heard what he said?

STEPHANIE. Yes, but I don't understand –

RHODA. Deborah, you –

DEBORAH. No! Stay out of it, both of you! Steffie dearest,
    I know this must be painful. It isn't that I don't want you to
    work for the good of the world, but not by being exploited. I
    agree, Colonel.

STEPHANIE. Please, what's going on?

DEBORAH. I won't have that.

RHODA. Why not? Those are the rules you live by, you and
    your consortium.

DEBORAH. I intend to change those rules. If caring about one
    young girl is a luxury then it is a luxury that I have access
    to. But it never was a luxury. All your schemes, your notions
    for a new world – if they harm one hair of one baby's head,
    then they are useless! (*To* HASSAN.) Not that I expect you
    to listen, who cares about domesticity . . . One girl? . . . poof!
    You are wrong.

HASSAN. But I agree.

DEBORAH. Oh do you! In any case, how long do you think
    you'll last? If you do you'll end up like the rest of them, a
    despot. How long before your best friend plots against you
    and – so sadly – you have to have him killed. Then the
    factions, the rule of terror, oh, so regrettable . . . All in the
    name of the people of course!

    But, if you're not blown to pieces . . . If you find enough
    hoods to protect you, pay them well enough, you'll survive
    to stage two. The arms deals, the gifts, the bribes rolling in –
    and everything to be fortified, to protect them.

    Every week another edict. Backed by guns.

RHODA. What? What's she –

DEBORAH. And there must be a Palace worthy of the status
    of the Leader! Roads to be renamed, useless projects under-
    taken by foreign investment –

RHODA. Well, we all know –

DEBORAH. New uniforms, of course . . . since you're now head of the army and the navy and every other bloody gang of criminals.

And you can have everything – anything! This man's daughter? – This man's wife? Yours!

And how on earth can that be enough. More means more. And more – more. And look! Look at the land to the north and to the south . . . rain forest and fertile sea plains. Weren't they part of the old kingdom once? Out with the maps . . . yes! You see? A thousand years ago this was all ours . . . Give it back! Justice for the People!

We're fed up. Fed up with you. The rest of us. The women. The children. The old, the sick. Those of us who don't fight. Who don't want to fight.

Steph? (*As* STEPHANIE *moans softly.*)

STEPHANIE. Sorry – (*She makes a dash for the exit.*)

RHODA (*assists her out*). Whoops – come on, quick.

They go. DEBORAH *makes to follow them.* HASSAN *restrains her.*

HASSAN. Please. Don't go. (*She stops, arrested by his tone.*) You are right. Do you think that I don't know that you are right? I have lived alone for seven years. My life was too dangerous. I could not risk someone close. Not one – individual.

He looks at her longingly, speaks softly.

My God, what can you not do for us? Hospitals, schools, roads . . . dear lady, think of it. Cool towns with libraries, theatres. Markets with food . . . Shops with dresses, furniture, tools . . . Even flowers.

DEBORAH. Please –

HASSAN. Listen to me, you who say you can make the desert flourish. Can you do this? Make fertile that which was barren? Create groves of fig and olive where there was only sand? Make fields of orange, pomegranate . . . eucalyptus, palm – where before was rock, shale?

DEBORAH. With the appropriate science, yes.

HASSAN. I need you.

DEBORAH (*backs off, mutters*). Don't.

HASSAN. I need you here – by my side.

DEBORAH. I can't

HASSAN. Very well, then we nationalise all mineral and oil resource. (*DEBORAH shakes her head, disbelieving.*) You think we cannot? This was said to Colonel Nasser, of the Canal. (*He comes close.*) Stay lady. Return the favours that the earth has disgorged for you. Your husband is dead, your child is grown. Time to choose.

DEBORAH. For once in my life I am doing just that.

HASSAN. Are you? Why go back to your pretty fields – they produce too much. Stay. Allow my people to buy that which you now feed to your cattle at a price we can afford. How can we live together when we have so little and you have so much? The world starves . . . And you grow daffodils. Come with me, to the refugee camps.

DEBORAH (*mutters*). I've read the reports. I've seen the films.

HASSAN. No. You have not seen. You have not smelt it. Children with teeth falling from their mouths . . . They smell so bad. Have you seen them bleeding through their pores? Have you felt those legs, those fat, blown stomachs? Do you think they die peacefully?

DEBORAH. Please don't.

HASSAN. How can you say what you will do and what you will not do? That you will go away –

DEBORAH. I am aware –

HASSAN. No. You are not aware. You are rich. You are not aware.

DEBORAH. Your accusations are unjust. The Pedersen Foundation has been of immense benefit to this country and

I hope it may continue to be so. Please release the necessary papers for my daughter to leave with me.

HASSAN (*he sounds tired*). I can't make you change your mind?

DEBORAH. What do you want from me?

HASSAN. Want? I need something unconditional.

DEBORAH. From me? Why? Why should I? What means did you use to gain power here? You think I want my child to bear a child here?!

HASSAN. Here   there   where is safe?

DEBORAH. Thanks to your vile weaponry –

But she collapses in tears. HASSAN *takes her in his arms.* DAVID *enters.*

DAVID (*clears his throat discreetly*). Sorry, wrong moment.

DEBORAH. David, I thought you were up country.

DAVID. Stephanie rang me. Look, I'm dreadfully sorry. We were going to tell you –

STEPHANIE (*rushes in, to* DAVID's *arms*). David! I've missed you!

DEBORAH. What?

DAVID. I know what you must think, Mrs. Pedersen –

STEPHANIE. But I seduced him – honestly! Darling, I want a family.

DAVID. It's what she wants. And Prime Minister Sa'id has offered me a job in communications. Dad owns a lot of TV companies and stuff so I can make myself useful.

STEPHANIE. Mummy –

DEBORAH. Why didn't you say?

STEPHANIE. I was going to. (*Excited.*) We've got an apartment –

DAVID. I've been buying some things –

STEPHANIE. What? Tell me . . . (*To her mother as she and* DAVID *go.*) Come for tea!

RHODA (*following them, to* DEBORAH). Could have told you. You only had to ask.

DEBORAH (*after silence*). I owe you an apology.

HASSAN. Not at all. She is too young for me.

DEBORAH. I'm not going to be held responsible for anything I agreed when I thought my daughter

HASSAN. No, no, no. Please, help me. These drawings . . . this is shit, is it not? Your ICI is trying to sell us pup? (*He draws her to the desk, displays drawings.*)

DEBORAH. What is it? (*Picks up a drawing.*) Ahh . . . yes!

HASSAN. They say we cannot make our houses as we have always done.

DEBORAH. No, of course you mustn't build mud houses, you waste valuable topsoil. (*She leans over the drawings.*) These are wonderful! As you see they can be built without skilled labour – these are decent houses . . . Bathrooms with plumbing –

HASSAN. And paper roof!

DEBORAH. Why not? Perfect insulation, the product of the latest technology.

HASSAN. Suitable for primitive culture. Let me tell you, culture responds to technology. I, Hassan , say no to this insult. A technology designed for a poor country is a poor technology.

DEBORAH. Totally false logic! Look at the perspectives! Yes, the walls are made of composite but the houses appear utterly traditional. And when it says expanded paper roofs, what is paper but wood exposed to the sophisticated technology you demand? (*He moves away from the desk, she follows.*) Please, I'm experienced in this field, I've worked on rehousing earthquake victims. This scheme could be repeated from the mountains to the sea.

HASSAN. And who will pay?

DEBORAH. Buildings give you collateral! Open a state bank, offer decent lending rates. Prime minister – people must have their own place. It's a matter of dignity. Home is where you begin . . . If that's not right . . . Even a rat has its own nest, what do you want, the Taj Mahal?

HASSAN. When you are angry you are very fine. Your skin glows like the dawn through alabaster. Very well . . . (*Throws down the drawings.*) . . . Build your bloody houses, may they fall down and crush you.

RHODA (*marches in, looms over HASSAN as he slumps at his desk*). Trees!

DEBORAH. Not now, Mother.

RHODA. I haven't got time to mess about. Hassan, I want a national tree policy. Trees give you water, shade, crops, clothing, fuel, shelter, fodder, furniture, herbs, seed, flowers, fruit, nuts, resin and humus. And stuffing. They air-condition the streets and give jobs to the old men, sweeping up. Sign here.

HASSAN. Old woman, we should listen to you. (*He signs the document.*)

RHODA *rolls up the paper, stumps off, followed by* DEBORAH.

DEBORAH (*going*). Mother, I really wish you wouldn't barge in and interrupt everything, you do it all the time! (*Bumps into* ALI.)

ALI. Pardon, Madame. (*He looks after the two women.*) These women. (HASSAN *murmurs.* ALI *sits as his desk across from* HASSAN.) I think you lust after this infidel.

HASSAN (*easily*). Laquelle, la mère ou la fille?

ALI (*in Arabic*). You don't fool me, oh scrapings from the bottom of a well.

HASSAN. Their presence offends you?

ALI. Why else are they here, getting in the way?

HASSAN. Oh, these middle-class Englishwomen work harder than mules. When we are ready – phhtt!!

ALI (*going*). We should have taken the jobs with Radio Casablanca.

HASSAN (*calls*). I agree! (*To himself.*) We would have earned more.

He bends to his work. A pause. He looks up at a sound.

DEBORAH. My valise. I left it here.

HASSAN. You are not leaving?

DEBORAH. I . . . I've deferred my departure.

HASSAN. Good. Very good. You look well.

DEBORAH. Thank you.

HASSAN. No – claustrophobia?

She shakes her head, smiles. He makes round the desk.

Please to remember that I, Hassan, am your devoted and loyal servant.

DEBORAH. You're not going to start all that again – ?

HASSAN. How can I help myself? I see your ankle on the stair, so white, so fine . . . I could snap it with my finger –

DEBORAH. Don't!

HASSAN. And your hair, the colour of pale fire in the dark desert night –

DEBORAH. If you go on like this –

HASSAN. What can I offer? For one glance of those emerald eyes I would give a thousand camels, in milk . . . ten thousand fine carpets for one evening, one night under the stars.

DEBORAH. Hang on. There is something.

HASSAN. Anything that your heart desires, beloved iris of the mountains.

DEBORAH. Lavatories. I need lavatories. Three dozen, portable, site workers for the use of.

HASSAN. It is true. You have no soul.

DEBORAH. By tomorrow.

HASSAN. Alas, not my department.

DEBORAH. Your signature will do.

HASSAN. Very well. If I may kiss the palm of your hand.

DEBORAH. You may. For two hundred tents. I need them for the labourers.

HASSAN. I pay.

DEBORAH. You are liberality itself.

HASSAN. And so I shall prove. (*Kisses the palm of her hand.*)

DEBORAH. We'll see. We'll see about that.

HASSAN. Yes. You look well.

DEBORAH. You too.

HASSAN. Thank you, Mrs. Pedersen.

DEBORAH. Deborah.

HASSAN. Thank you, Deborah.

DEBORAH. Thank you, Colonel – Prime Minister.

HASSAN. Hassan.

DEBORAH (*demurely*). Thank you, Hassan.

They smile at each other.

End.